Complete Book
of Rehearsal Techniques
for the High School Orchestra

Complete Book
of Rehearsal Techniques
for the High School Orchestra

Irvin Gattiker

Parker Publishing Company, Inc.   West Nyack, New York

Library of Congress Cataloging in Publication Data

Gattiker, Irvin,
    Complete book of rehearsal techniques for the high
school orchestra.

    1. Orchestra. 2. School music--Instruction and
study. 3. Conducting. I. Title. II. Title:
Rehearsal techniques for the high school orchestra.
MT730.G35   785'.06'6   77-8229
ISBN 0-13-158212-7

Printed in the United States of America

TO MY WONDERFUL STUDENTS THROUGHOUT THE YEARS
WHO HAVE MADE IT ALL WORTHWHILE

WHAT THIS BOOK WILL DO FOR YOU

More than thirty years of teaching and conducting orchestras, working with my own groups, and watching and listening to other orchestras in rehearsal made me realize that there is a need for this book. I do not mean that the majority of the groups I have heard were inferior; this is far from true, and over the years I have been thrilled by innumerable outstanding groups heard in performance.

Rather, this book is written with the hope that through the application of the guidelines I present, your rehearsals may become even more efficient and productive. If the technique of rehearsing can be streamlined and a greater amount of time and effort channeled into the development of the total musical effect and interpretation, more will be accomplished with less expenditure of energy and with fewer jitters at concert time.

The recommendations I provide will serve as your guide to improved orchestral performance and better contest ratings. Through the use of these time-saving rehearsal devices you will be able to cover a great deal of material, thereby giving your students a well-rounded musical foundation for performance.

I have selected and covered the most important areas pertaining to orchestra rehearsal techniques. Not only will this book help you plan the very first rehearsal, but you will also find, in Chapter 7, thirteen specific guides for productive subsequent rehearsals. Among the objectives for a good rehearsal are the improvement of tone quality and correct rhythm. How to achieve these is dealt with in detail.

Since orchestras are made up of human beings, personnel and discipline problems will arise at times. Chapter 9 gives you tested techniques for preventing and coping with these difficulties.

Many high schools, as part of their total program, present musical shows with much success. To help you in preparing this type of program, a chapter on this has been included. Also, at times, the instrumental director may conduct choral groups and/or soloists with his orchestra, and so a very useful chapter is devoted to this particular situation.

In Chapter 13, rehearsal guides for two selected orchestral works are presented to assist you in applying many of the techniques described in the earlier chapters. One is from the baroque period and the other is a 20th Century composition; each is examined for its individual problems, and the ways to solve them most effectively are described in detail.

The appendices contain tested warm-up drills and seating arrangements, as well as a transposition table and instrumental substitutions. This reference material should prove to be very useful to you.

Human nature, as a rule, is reluctant to change; the idea that what was done by the past generation is ''good enough'' still exists and traditions die hard. However, often there may be a more efficient way of doing things. Basic routines can be put to good advantage if applied in a new and stimulating manner, often saving time and bringing improved results. I know your problems, and the suggestions I give here are not just theories that look good on paper; they have been tested and found to be successful by myself and by many other experienced orchestra directors. However, they are not the only ones possible; other practical ideas, no doubt, will come to your mind and should be added to those listed. While this handbook is especially directed toward the experienced conductor, beginners will also find it a useful guide.

In many respects, the conductor is the world's greatest clock-watcher. You will agree, I'm sure, that there is never enough time for rehearsing. The constant feeling that the clock on the wall is looking over your shoulder is a circumstance with which you and I must live. This book will show you how to utilize your time more effectively and efficiently and will provide you with all the tools and techniques you need to do just that.

Irvin Gattiker

ACKNOWLEDGMENTS

A book of this type is difficult to write without some assistance from colleagues. I am especially grateful to the following people for reading portions of the manuscript and for their constructive help: Dr. Karl D. Ernst, Emeritus Professor of Music, California State University, Hayward, California; Mr. A. Verne Wilson, Supervisor of Music, Portland Public Schools, Portland, Oregon; and Dr. Wendal S. Jones, Professor of Music, Eastern Washington State College, Cheney, Washington.

TABLE OF CONTENTS

11

Chapter 1

Selecting and Developing an Efficient Rehearsal Schedule

It is very important that ample thought and consideration be given by music directors and the administrative staff to the problem of rehearsal scheduling. A fine organization will be less effective if rehearsals are at a poor time. Some of the advantages and disadvantages of various scheduling arrangements will be discussed in this chapter.

The attempt to fit instrumental music into the demands of the traditional subjects' scheduling explains to some extent the variation found in the number of orchestral rehearsals per week. It is important that the music department and the administration cooperate and endeavor to understand each other's problems in regard to scheduling. Situations vary, but sometimes an unfavorable one can be changed *if the director presents the benefits* of a different arrangement to his administrators.

MORNING VS. AFTERNOON

In a high school large enough to have a band and an orchestra, both should be scheduled during the morning hours, if possible. Of course, the Social Studies, Science, Math, and English instructors will say that the early hours are best for *their* classes also, and to this we must agree. However, there is more to this than one might expect. Music requires split-second coordination of mind, eyes, and hands, at least as much as any subject taught and generally more than most. It is best, therefore, that the student rehearse while he is fresh and alert and has lots of energy in store. Of course, if there is no other time available for one reason or another, having orchestra rehearsals in the afternoon is better than not having an orchestra at all.

Some people will argue that concerts are usually given in the evening and that students must be alert then, so why should rehearsals be in the morning? This can be answered in several ways:

1. Although the players do have to be alert the concert is not a learning situation.
2. It is always a good idea to allow some rest between rehearsals and performances. A warm-up period should be held before the concert, if possible, but the performers should not be tired out from a late afternoon rehearsal. This is especially true for wind players.
3. Concerts are generally in the evening in order to have public attendance not because this is better for the players—it isn't.
4. In many high schools there are now seven or more periods, and some students leave early because of employment. These people could not be members of a musical organization if it met during the last period.
5. There is a definite disadvantage in rehearsing immediately after lunch, because of the difficulties encountered by wind players blowing right after eating.

ADVANTAGES OF COINCIDING
WITH BAND PERIOD

If the high school has both a band and orchestra with different directors, a good plan is to have them scheduled at the same time. Many schools, however, are not large enough to have sufficient wind players to supply both groups. If the band and orchestra are scheduled at different times, it is quite often impossible for wind players to belong to both groups and still schedule other subjects. In some cases the school could not have an orchestra unless it were scheduled at the same time as the band, and the students would miss the exposure to the different music and techniques of orchestral playing. Usually if there are two instrumental music organizations, the school is large enough to have two separate rehearsal rooms.

With band and orchestra scheduled during the same period, the following program of rehearsals would be possible: Full band three days per week. During the other two days the first chair wind players report to orchestra. This allows the band director to work with the remaining students on details which, in most cases, the first chair people have already mastered. In the long run, this will make for a superior band, as any performing organization is only as good as its combined talent. This arrangement permits having three days for string orchestra literature and detailed string work on full orchestra selections. Also, sectional string work or small ensembles can be scheduled whenever desired.

Many schools have full orchestra only once a week. While the wind parts can be learned in this manner, one full rehearsal a week is not really adequate for proper work on balance, tone color, and general interpretation. As a result, the orchestra may sound as if it is ''just playing notes.'' Of course during the football season, if the band is practicing marching routines, the cooperation of the orchestra director may pay off in both good rapport and more full orchestra time later.

If There Is Only One Director

If a school district hires just one director for band and orchestra, the above plan obviously will not work. Although some musicians are capable of doing fine work in handling both groups in a school situation, many lean toward one or the other and one organization may suffer. However, in many school districts it may be possible to have only one director for both, and if he is a well-prepared musician willing to work diligently at mastering the problems of the organization with which he is less familiar, this situation can work out very well. I know of a great many such cases.

One disadvantage of having full orchestra five days a week is that there is very little time for detailed string work without the winds becoming bored. Sometimes schedules can be worked out so that the wind players have a library period one or two days a week or they can practice or have ensembles if rooms are available. Some string work is always necessary since the string parts are usually rather challenging.

TRADITIONAL OR FLEXIBLE SCHEDULE?

The length of the period will, in most cases, determine the length of the rehearsal. This usually is about 50 minutes; any less time is ineffective. The rehearsal period should be on a five-day basis. Keep in mind too that any instrumental group does not get a full 50 minutes. There is tuning, stopping for instructional comments, making announcements, etc. Also, the rehearsal must end a few minutes early to allow the musicians time to put their instruments away. All players have certain routine tasks to perform in caring for their instruments; they should always be given adequate time for this and to get to their next class.

During the past several years many schools have departed somewhat from the traditional concept of one period per day per subject (with a six-period day), and have begun to implement more flexible programs. With the aid of computers, rather complex schedules can be worked out easier than if they had to be done manually. Following are some approaches to the problem of scheduling rehearsals:

—At Bend High School in Bend, Oregon, for example, a flexible schedule was employed from 1959 to 1975, wherein orchestra was held four days per week with periods of either 55 minutes or 90 minutes. Teachers could request the time when they wanted their classes extended. The schedule was made up one week in advance so teachers and students knew ahead of time what the next week's procedure would be. The entire school was involved and computer scheduling was utilized. The administrators were in favor of the program, but at the beginning of the fall term, 1975, the school returned to a more conventional type of scheduling due to budget considerations.

The school now operates on a mini-period day with 45-minute periods. Orchestra and band are at different times, with orchestra the last period in the day. In this way, the wind players can schedule orchestra during ninth period, but can leave if a string rehearsal is to be held. Mr. Robert Shotwell, the orchestra director, preferred the previous, flexible type of program.

—At Sammamish High School in Bellevue, Washington, full orchestra has been held once a week in a pre-school rehearsal (7-7:50 a.m.) for one year. For the past two years, string rehearsals have been held daily at the same time as ensemble class, making possible mixed ensembles and baroque, classical, and chamber orchestra. Sometimes these are full string rehearsals, sometimes sections, with artist clinicians used on a limited basis to coach sections. (These are limited because of finances.)

Mr. Normand Poulshock, the director, says of the program: "The 7:00 a.m. rehearsal was relatively successful and allowed us to prepare, as well as one might expect with one rehearsal per week, a few numbers for concerts and for a clinic at the state convention. Transportation was a bit of a problem—I picked up some of the students myself on the way to school.

"We are continuing the scheduling of orchestra opposite ensembles as it works well. Next year, due to increased school enrollment, we will be on an eight-period day and are scheduling band, ensembles, and orchestra at the same time as the three lunch periods. This may allow us further flexibility."

— The Columbus, Ohio secondary schools operate on a nine-period day, 40 minutes a period:

The nine-period day has been very successful in the Columbus junior and senior high schools and has offered the following advantages:

1. The problem of long lunch periods is eliminated.
2. Pupils are able to elect more nonacademic subjects than were previously possible.
3. From the principal's point of view, music scheduling is easier.

Significantly, these advantages in the Columbus schedule are making it possible to build a strong music program.

How does the scheduling work? In the case of instrumental music, it has been found that large performing groups must dictate the scheduling. The administrators feel that they are the most important single-period subjects in the school day; therefore, these groups are scheduled first.

Single conflict subjects (that is, only one period of each is offered in the curriculum) are programmed next. They include subjects such as physics, trigonometry, advanced theory, and third-year shorthand. Classes that can meet two or more times a day are then scheduled. (Incidentally, the nine-period day allows three periods per day for subjects that conflict.)

A wide range of music electives is possible under a nine-period day plan. Using this schedule, ten periods of music per week are considered a reasonable number for a pupil. Fifteen may be scheduled with permission, and in exceptional cases eighteen periods are permitted, although not recommended since there are other subjects worthy of election.

In the Columbus program, secondary music teachers are requested to submit to the principal lists of pupils for preliminary scheduling in specific music groups such as band, orchestra, choir and boys' and girls' choruses and ensembles.

The choral schedule is set up to avoid conflicts with the major instrumental groups at the school. Consideration is given to the idea of selecting periods when most of the students are available.

The class in general music, the ninth period, is called "junior choir" to erase the stigma attached to the phrase "general music."[1]

—In Missoula, Montana, the two high schools, Sentinel and Hellgate, have a nine-period day. The orchestra rehearsal starts out with strings alone for a 45-minute period on Monday. On Tuesday they have two 45-minute periods back-to-back. The first 45 minutes are used for ensembles of various combinations, and the second for full orchestra. On Wednesday and Friday the schedule is the same as on Monday; on Thursday, the same as Tuesday. The next week it is reversed, and the strings are alone on Tuesday and Thursday. This routine of alternate days is maintained throughout the year; thus, in a period of two weeks each group (strings and full orchestra) has five rehearsals. Mr. Harold Herbig, the director, finds this schedule very satisfactory.

—In Portland, Oregon, the Stanford School Scheduling System has been implemented at John Marshall High School:

A very brief overview of the Marshall program will attempt to show some of the advantages in scheduling by using computer data processing designs. A brief explanation of the instrumental music and art courses will illustrate actual possibilities for improving teaching and learning in the fine arts.

In planning the Marshall program the teachers structured their courses in the most effective manner they could conceive without the

---

[1]Robert H. Klotman, ed., *Scheduling Music Classes* (Reston, Va., formerly Washington, D.C.: Music Educators National Conference, 1968), pp. 20-22.

traditional restrictions of one hour, one teacher, and thirty students. Working within the parameters of twenty-one 20-minute modules, or periods, per day—comprising a weekly cycle of 105 modules—the staff created varying course structures forming small groups of six to fifteen students, laboratory-size groups varying from twenty to seventy students, and large groups of up to 375 with class time ranging from one module in the foreign language laboratory to six modules in one of the science laboratories. The number of meetings per week in any one course ranged from one to six. They created over forty teaching teams of two to six members, expanded the use of audio-visual resources, utilized services of twelve paraprofessionals, and established resource study centers (departmental libraries).

Perhaps the most important concept underlining the Marshall program is "independent study." Students average approximately one-third of their school time outside of classes. During this time a student may do generally assigned homework, but beyond that may plan and carry out special study projects of his own selection, meeting his unique needs, interests, and capabilities. All students, regardless of academic ability, have the opportunity for these experiences. The results have been truly gratifying to the staff. Original, creative projects beyond the expected performance of the student are continually being submitted with many crossing subject lines into two or more curricular areas. Individual teacher and student conferencing within the school day is an important part of the independent study program and is essential for quality independent study projects.

Modular Schedule for Music

A look at the structure of the instrumental program at Marshall will serve to indicate some of the advantages of a computerized modular schedule in the music area. The course structure as developed by the instrumental music teacher indicates the entire senior band as a unit meets three times a week for three modules (one hour) each time. In addition, the woodwinds meet once separately for three modules, as do the high brass, low brass, and percussion. Thus the instructor meets four separate subgroups of the band in addition to the entire group. Each student in the senior band meets with the instructor for 220 minutes a week. The student can also spend a varying number of modules, according to his needs, working independently in the practice rooms. The intermediate band, beginning orchestra, and advanced orchestra are also structured in somewhat the same manner with small homogeneous subgroups meeting separately in addition to two or three meetings as an entire unit.[2]

Among the advantages of a computerized modular program is

---

[2]Klotman, *Scheduling Music Classes*, pp. 31-32.

one which is of particular significance to those concerned with the elective and fine arts areas. Experience of the several schools in the Stanford Project indicates that students on the average take one more subject in modular programs than in a conventional program. The additional subject being an elective has made it possible for more students (usually average and above in ability) to have worthwhile experiences in the fine arts. This is a development which music educators and others heartily support.[3]

The above excerpts are from the article, "Data Processing and Program Planning" by Gaynor Petrequin who was principal at John Marshall High School until he became Area II Field Administrator for the Portland Public Schools. I talked with Dr. Petrequin personally and his current evaluation of the program is as follows:

Through the years the innovative concepts implemented at Marshall High School have been modified as experience seemed to indicate in order to meet new demands and expectations. The overall process goal has always been and continues to be to individualize and humanize teaching and learning. The modular variable program with its attendant innovative components provides the means to achieve that end.

I also talked with Mr. Ralph Salyard who was orchestra director at Marshall High School for 12 years. He says of the program,

It is especially good for music. It opens up opportunities for sectionals and ensembles that might not be possible with conventional scheduling.

KEY REASONS FOR SECTIONALS

Much of the success and musical achievement of your orchestra will depend upon regularly including sectional rehearsals. If the strings regularly meet alone part of the time, this is a sectional rehearsal; however, it is very often advantageous to have the first and second violins alone for part of a period and also the violas and cellos alone. At times, even a short, one-section rehearsal can be helpful. Usually the woodwinds, brass, and percussion will not require as much sectional work as the strings, but sometimes it is necessary.

Five Important Justifications for Sectionals

1. Many conductors work, without much success, at trying to gain that "extra something" that makes a finished performance. It is often

---

[3]Klotman, *Scheduling Music Classes*, p. 33.

possible to obtain this desired result in a single practice of the separate sections.

2. Sectionals will better acquaint the conductor with all parts of the score, the importance of every instrument and the relationship of the various parts to the entire composition.

3. Errors in intonation, rhythm, attacks, phrasing, balance, dynamics, and interpretation that slip by unnoticed in the full rehearsal will become more obvious to the players and the director. These can be dealt with more effectively in a sectional than in the full group rehearsal.

4. Sectionals will allow each player to be heard more distinctly than when in the full group. However, individuals should not be asked to play alone unless it is a solo passage or a demonstration of something done very well. Playing faults can be noted and discussed in private. Usually individual problems can be corrected reasonably well as they are pointed out and rehearsed by the section.

5. Sectionals save time in perfecting a selection. It is possible, and most desirable, to have more than one sectional at the same time, provided that ample room is available. In such an arrangement, an assistant conductor is necessary. High school students are not mature enough to rehearse by themselves. (Ensembles, yes, with some help, but not a whole section.)

Many times an outstanding student from the section will be able to lead the sectional. I have found that this has several advantages. It enables this person to put to use his talents of pitch, rhythm, and technique. With some private help from you in score reading and conducting techniques, this will be excellent practice if he is interested in becoming a music director himself. Even if he does not have this specifically in mind, he can find out what goes into being a director and whether or not he might like to do this sort of thing. Another advantage is that students often enjoy working under a peer, and will, at times, work harder than usual.

Some directors are fortunate in having teacher aides available, or sometimes a student from a nearby college doing practice teaching can take over a sectional.

A bonus in sectionals can be the students' discovery of melodies that are sometimes covered by the sound of the full orchestra. They can be made aware of these interesting parts and effective ways can be found to bring them out.

ORGANIZING SECTIONAL
REHEARSALS EFFICIENTLY

Having discussed the reasons why sectional rehearsals are necessary, here are eight key points on organizing these rehearsals:

1. Plan sectionals in advance and inform the players. If a portion of the rehearsal is to be with the complete group, the sectional should be first, with the full orchestra rehearsal following. This will put together what was taken apart earlier. Experience has shown that putting the whole together during the same period while it is still "hot" does wonders for morale. The worked-over spots are still fresh in the minds of the players and that part of the composition worked on should sound considerably better. This acts as a psychological lift for the group, since they can see the value of intense concentration on difficult sections. If the period is only 45-50 minutes, only one or two selections can be worked on, but doing this as often as necessary will pay off.

2. Whenever possible, tell your students in advance which portions are to be worked over during the coming sectional. This will give them an opportunity to go over the material—already a step toward improvement. They no doubt know the weak spots, but, human nature being what it is, they tend to put off actually working them out. Advance notice that these spots will be tackled will get them moving in the right direction.

3. Plan *exactly* what is to be worked on and what you want to accomplish during the sectional. These details should isolate measures that have proven to be difficult or have not been mastered.

4. Put such trouble spots on the chalkboard, marking any changes of articulation, bowing, or fingering that might be helpful in bringing about improvement. Rhythmic problems can also be illustrated. A good example is the following:

Figure 1-1a   Figure 1-1b

The triplet form is often played incorrectly as Figure 1-1b. Place Figure 1-1a on the board, then the solution as shown in Figure 1-2:

Figure 1-2

The "o" is silent and the rhythm is 1-let, 2-let. Have the players say aloud together, "1-o-let, 2-o-let," etc., and then on cue omit the "o," but keep the tempo and rhythm the same, ending as "1-let, 2-let."

5. If band and orchestra meet at the same time, string rehearsals are held several days each week, and this takes care of their sectionals. When wind rehearsals are indicated, the string players can work in ensembles, practice individually or in small groups, or study for that part of the period. They can have a sectional or part-sectional if another person is available to conduct. Sometimes a mini-sectional can be held at the end of the period with the others being excused a few minutes early. (This will only work if discipline is such that the others will pack up and sit or leave quietly.)

    Wind rehearsals can be held before school, during an activity period, or after school, if no other time is available. I prefer having all the winds together in a sectional as a rule; however, there may be times when it is advantageous to separate the brass and woodwinds for some specific workout if there are rooms and personnel available for this.

6. In wind sectionals it is not necessary for the players to sit in the normal orchestral positions. I gather them around me as closely as possible, placing the woodwinds on my left and the brass on the right as in Figure 1-3.

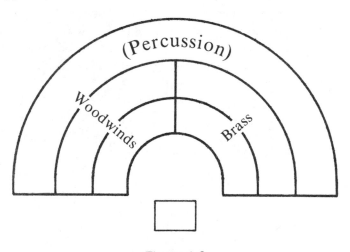

Figure 1-3

If wind and string sectionals are going at the same time, it is best to leave the strings in the regular rehearsal room, due to the larger numbers involved. The winds can be moved to a smaller room, since these players can sit closer together.

7. If you are in the fortunate position of having a teacher aide, student teacher, or other interested adult to assist you during the sectional, this helps immeasurably. He or she can move about the room helping individuals with some special problems or sit in a section and play along while a difficult spot is worked out. (Sometimes an aide is available only to conduct one sectional while you direct the other; however, if he or she can also be present at full rehearsals, the individual or sectional help given can be of real benefit.)

8. Never let sectional rehearsals go until the last minute before a performance. The groundwork on details must be done early in the time period. There may be an isolated instance when some last-minute corrections must be worked out, but these can usually be taken care of within the full group—there shouldn't be anything extensive to be done at that time.

HOW OFTEN SHOULD
STRINGS REHEARSE ALONE?

The string section is the foundation of the orchestra. To achieve the sheer beauty of sound for which they are noted, and because of the velocity of execution, strings need much practice together.

Upon examining any orchestral score suitable for high school players, one finds that the string parts are usually the most difficult. Not only are the players required to perform very rapid passages, but at times long, slow, legato tones are indicated. In addition to many changes of position in the fingering, many different bow techniques are also necessary. Legato, staccato, spiccato, détaché, portato, martelé, and sul ponticello must all be mastered by the high school string player. It is therefore necessary that you include some time for strings alone in your rehearsal schedule. A safe minimum would be the equivalent of two full periods a week. Where a third can be included, so much the better.

As stated earlier, if orchestra and band are scheduled simultaneously, your string rehearsal time is built into the schedule. If not, suggestions have also been given previously as to what the winds can do during string rehearsal time. Each of us has to find a practical solution to the scheduling problems of our particular situation. We are all aware of the importance of rehearsing with the strings alone, not only on the regular orchestra music, but on special string techniques. Also, the players should be exposed to the beauty of string literature. *It is essential that some time during each week the strings work alone.*

WHEN TO SCHEDULE SMALL ENSEMBLES

The formation of small ensembles should be among your highest priorities.

These ensembles can include duets, trios, quartets, quintets, octets and larger ensembles of twelve or so. You will find an adequate supply of music for all combinations.

Ensembles are great learning situations. Usually there is only one player on a part, which makes each dependent upon himself and not on the player next to him. From no other source can a student learn the art of balance so well.

The problem will be when to schedule rehearsals for these groups. Again, each particular situation will dictate, to some extent, the best time. Sometimes a different ensemble rehearsal can be scheduled each day about 45 minutes before the first period class. This may present some problems, however, if bus transportation is involved.

Another way to hold rehearsal is at the last period of the day. Ensemble can be a regularly scheduled class under this plan, and students who don't have to leave early for employment or to go on a bus can sign up. String ensembles can meet, say, three times a week and woodwind, brass, or percussion twice a week. Or strings can meet Tuesday and Thursday, woodwinds on Monday, brass on Wednesday and percussion on Friday. The latter three can rehearse on Monday, Wednesday, and Friday at the same time, if desired, and you can work with each group a portion of the time.

If your school has an activity period, ensembles can meet then. What better time for this than a period set aside for students to work in their particular area of interest?

The least effective schedule, but sometimes the only option open, is to have ensemble rehearsal after school. Again, bus transportation may dictate, to some degree, which students are able to participate.

If there are different directors for orchestra and band, the band director usually takes care of the wind and percussion ensembles. In this situation I have found that the following schedule works well: String rehearsals Mondays and Wednesdays and full orchestra on Tuesdays and Thursdays. Devote Friday's regular period to string ensembles for the orchestra director and the other ensembles for the band director, spending part of the time with each group. Large ensembles rehearse in the regular rehearsal room (with a conductor) and other small ensembles work alone or with an aide or student assistant. Early morning and/or after school rehearsals can be reserved for the "extra" practice needed prior to a performance or contest. The students usually don't mind coming those few extra minutes.

It is not always possible to work all the students into ensembles. Those not participating can practice by themselves if rooms are available, study, or mend, sort, mark, or file music. It is good for them to listen to the ensembles at times and take in the suggestions given, so that they will know some of the problems and subtleties involved when they start small ensemble work.

Chapter 2

Practical Guidelines for Conducting Tryouts and Placement

It is totally unfair to both an inadequate player and the ensemble he wishes to join to allow him to become a part of it. Not only will the player become discouraged and probably drop out, but the performance standard of the group will also suffer. Worse, he may never wish to continue with his instrument after a bad experience of trying to keep up. Far better to try him out. If he cannot pass the tryout ask him to continue studying and try again next semester or thereafter until he succeeds. This is a positive approach; the director is telling him that sooner or later he expects him to be successful.

The director must have an idea of how well a new student plays and where to place him. This can hardly be done effectively while he plays with the group. The director cannot, at that time, give him 100% of his attention. So an audition is necessary in this situation, too.

The audition also establishes a feeling of the importance of the orchestra. It presents a challenge to a player, something to strive for and to be permitted to join provided qualifications are met. It is selective, but open to all who can pass a tryout.

THE MAKE-UP OF AN EFFECTIVE
TRYOUT BLANK

The tryout blank or form should include all of the information that will be helpful to the director. Dittoed or mimeographed sheets should be available in ample supply at the end of the school year for use before school opens again in the fall. There should also be some available during the year if new students enter the school. If a director is new to a school he should check on this and if there are no such blanks he should get some made up early enough to use two to three weeks ahead of the opening of school.

There are many items that could be included on a tryout blank, but the eight listed in Figure 2-1 are the most essential ones.

EIGHT SPECIFIC ITEMS
A TRYOUT SHOULD INCLUDE

The items listed on the form (Figure 2-1) are in a specific order with intonation first and musicianship last. By the time the tryout is over, a student will have had an opportunity through playing the various things to exhibit his musicianship.

Intonation and rhythmic accuracy are essential, of course, for every player, the latter especially so for percussionists.

Players should be able to play scales in the most used keys from memory. In the case of wind players, the director should ask for one or two scales in the sharp keys, since much orchestral music is not in the flat keys as is the case with most band music. The director may find that wind players need to practice up on unfamiliar keys.

Bowing and finger techniques in the strings should be carefully observed. The ability (or lack of ability) to play in the higher positions will determine to a large extent in which section of the violins a player should be placed. The difficulty of the music a lower string player can handle effectively will be determined also by how well he executes these positions. This is especially true for cello and bass players.

In the winds, the articulation is as important as bowing and fingering in the strings. Correct breathing and use of the tongue will make a great difference between an ordinary and an outstanding performance. It is assumed that any wind players who try out for orchestra will have fingering facility and will be aware of some of the alternate fingerings or positions for their particular instruments.

Much orchestra music does not require percussion other than tympani, but for the numbers that do it is important that percussion players be very precise. If the school has separate orchestra and band directors and the groups meet at the same time, there is usually no problem in getting good percussion players when needed. Many times I have enrolled pianists who were needed occasionally when a piano part was indicated, and instructed them on tympani and other percussion instruments on which they could double. Sometimes I have used one

TRYOUT FORM

(Name of High School)

Name _____ Date _____

Address _____ Phone _____

Parents' Name _____

Address _____ Phone _____

Year in school _____

Instrument _____

Private study:　　Yes _____ No _____ How long? _____

Do you plan to go to college?　　Yes _____ No _____

If yes, will you continue music?　　Yes _____ No _____

	1 A	2 B	3 or C	4 D	5 E
1. Intonation 　　Comment:					
2. Rhythmic accuracy 　　Comment:					
3. Scales 　　Comment:					
4. Strings:　Bowing technique 　　　　　　Finger technique 　　Comment:					
5. Winds—Articulation 　　Comment:					
6. Percussion—Rudiments 　　Comment:					
7. Sight-reading 　　Comment:					
8. Musicianship 　　Comment:					
General comments:					

Figure 2-1

or two string players as extra percussionists on a number that had several percussion parts.

Sight-reading will tell the director very quickly how the student does under pressure. Is he able to quickly establish the key and time signatures and pick up accidentals that may be lurking in the measures ahead? Does he play beat by beat, or seem to look ahead to get the overall phrasing? Is he able to make corrections quickly and avoid the same mistake the next time should a similar passage occur?

It will become obvious to the reader that tone quality has been omitted from the checklist. No player should be excluded because he does not possess excellent tone quality. Nor should he be "passed" if he happens to own a very fine instrument but is weak in all other factors on the list. Tone quality should be considered within the group as a whole.

From the information contained on the blank and from the audition itself, the director will be able to know enough about the student and his playing ability to make an accurate evaluation of his qualifications for participation in the group. The possible growth of the student must always be included in the evaluation. If he is on the borderline, he should be given a trial period with the orchestra. Many times, that one bit of confidence on the part of the director will carry the player over the top. The increased enthusiasm and extra practice needed to meet the requirements will usually do the rest.

WHEN TO SCHEDULE THE TRYOUTS

At least two weeks before classes begin, the director should obtain a list of all students who signed up for orchestra. This will tell him immediately of any new students who are hoping or planning to join the group. This can be done earlier if desired and if the office has the lists made up. If the director is new to the school, he can get a roster from the previous year and check for new people.

Sometimes when new people move into the area during the summer, inquiries concerning the orchestra are made and the director may be contacted earlier.

Having obtained addresses and phone numbers of the new students, contact should be made either by phone or form letter. I personally feel that a phone call is more direct and interesting, but either would be appropriate. After welcoming the student, the tryout policy should be explained and dates set for an informal meeting and for the audition itself. The student should be told to be prepared to play something he knows (not necessarily memorized) and some scales, and that he will be given some sight-reading.

Arrange an Informal Meeting

It is useful to meet with all newcomers, whether the number be only two or several, a day or two before the tryout. This informal get-together, if held at the school's music department, will allow the director to "show off" his music facilities and, best of all, observe his new "clients" informally. In fact, part one of the tryout has already begun—the observation of the personality of the young musician. It enables the students to meet the director under more relaxed circumstances than if the first meeting is at the actual audition. Also, the director can answer any questions that might be troubling the prospective players. Such a meeting need not be lengthy, but should be long enough to establish a sense of association with the department and to show the students that there is interest toward them on the part of the director.

Time and Place

The best time for the tryout is mid to late morning and the best place to hold it is in the high school orchestra room. The student is surrounded by music stands, staffed chalkboard, instruments, etc. These can help him relax because, to some extent, he is "protected" by these musical elements. He does not feel that he is the sole occupant of the room. Having the audition in the 10-12 A.M. time bracket will allow for some practice at home before appearing, yet he can "get it over with" before noon and need not fret about it until late in the day. The longer a student must wait, the more nervous he may become.

WHAT SHOULD YOU EXPECT
FROM THE PLAYERS?

It goes without saying that the director will expect both good and not-so-good playing during the tryout. He will have to exercise good judgment in deciding how much of the weakness is due to nervousness and how much due to lack of training and carelessness. Allowing at least 10-15 minutes per tryout will help in making a wise decision, as the first minutes are usually the hardest for the player. Many times a student is able to control himself better as he goes along. This is one reason I always place the sight-reading last; usually the student is more composed by then.

Take Stage Fright Into Consideration

In my experience, there have been a few times when a player simply could not continue because of extreme nervousness. The solution was simply to excuse the player and ask him to return at a later time, with an understanding remark that I also had gone through tryouts in my younger days and knew exactly how it felt. With few exceptions, the next time around the player came through with flying colors, simply because of a second chance and a feeling of being understood by the director.

In most cases each player will try to do his best or he would not even be at the tryout. Whenever possible, a few positive remarks will help send him on his way to enjoy the rest of the day.

THE TRYOUT PROCEDURE, STEP-BY-STEP

Having met with the prospective student or students prior to the tryout day will make the meeting that day easier, since everyone will already know everyone else. Giving each student a few minutes by himself in a practice room, if available, will give him a chance to rest, compose himself, and warm up a bit if he wishes. This will help him get in the mood for playing.

Here, then, is the step-by-step procedure for the tryout:

1. Brief greeting and collection of the tryout blank that was given out at the informal meeting.
2. Ask the student to tune up and warm up a bit in the manner he uses in preparation for practicing. This is actually part of the tryout. While he tunes and goes through a bit of a warm-up, the director can be unobtrusively listening to intonation, watching bow control, articulation in the winds, or rhythm with percussionists.
3. Ask him to play a portion of the prepared work about which he was informed earlier. If he feels more comfortable sitting, let that be his choice. After all, he sits while playing in orchestra (except percussion players). Here the director can observe intonation, rhythmic accuracy, bowing, articulation, etc.
4. Next he should play some scales, one of which should be in a minor key. Often two scales will be enough. This will tell the director something about his private study. In the strings, two octaves should be played, three on violin, if possible (to judge position competence); in the winds, one or two octaves.
5. Give the student several lines of sight-reading, having marked the music as to where to begin and stop. Allow him a minute or two to look it over and "hear" the music. He can establish the key and time signatures in his mind, as well as tempo marking and such things as staccato, legato, etc., for execution of the music. Ask him to play it at a reasonable tempo—one at which he feels comfortable. It is not necessary that he perform it at the exact tempo marking. Observe that which is good and pass over the rest. Make note of the things that are done well and remember that this, in all probability, will be the weakest part of the entire audition. Students will usually be able to learn a part through continual practice. The sight-reading is mainly to see what the player can do on the spot.
6. Thank the student and inform him then and there of your evaluation, or tell him that you will call him later that day. I've found that informing a

student at least the same day is best. Why should he be kept in suspense any longer?

Before going on to the next player, time should be taken to jot down any special comments.

HOW TO PLACE THE PLAYERS

The placing of players may bring about some complications if the judgment of merit is not fair and just in the eyes of the students.

If the director has the elementary or junior high orchestras that feed into his high school group, he will already know the ability of the players and can judge where to place them. If another director handles the lower school groups, he will recommend the students, but the high school director himself should visit the groups in the spring and listen to them, paying particular attention to the people who will be entering high school in the fall. If the director is new to the school, he can have the students sit the way they sat at the end of the previous year, filling in the gaps left by the seniors who graduated. He can then place the new players where he feels they may fit in. At the first rehearsal the director can announce that seating will be temporary for the time being and explain that he may move people about a little during the first month.

What About Seniority?

The question of seniority always arises, which many directors feel should prevail if at all possible. If a junior or sophomore is put ahead of a senior, the latter may lose interest and possibly withdraw from the group. Seniority gives the players some assurance and confidence that they have done well and are an asset to the group. They will usually work hard to maintain that standard.

Other directors feel that performance is the only criterion and do not worry too much about seniority. Most of the time the seniors are the best players because they have had more time in which to gain expertise and experience if they are at all serious about their music. If they are not anxious to work extremely hard, but enjoy playing, they may not be upset if others are placed ahead of them in the lineup.

Occasionally there may be a player who is definitely far ahead of the others, and the students may request that he be placed ahead of themselves without challenge. In this case the director must use his own judgment in making the final decision. Is this person really mature enough to handle the more responsible position even though his performance is superior? Is his personality well-adjusted enough that he will not let it "go to his head" and become difficult to work with? These are things to be considered.

One of my colleagues, Mr. Karl Spellman of Mark Morris High School, Longview, Washington, recently had a student who, without question, was the best player in the first violin section. With the consent of the others, the director decided to place her ahead as concertmaster. There were no problems. Everyone respected her superior ability, and when she was honored by being selected to perform a solo with the local symphony the other students were there to give her a standing ovation.

Strings

Since the string section makes up the bulk of the players, careful consideration must be given to seating here. By far the best method is to place a weak player next to a strong one, with the strong one on the outside. Finer ensemble will be attained and the skillful players will enjoy a sense of responsibility in aiding the less advanced performers. Also, the weaker players will gain confidence and begin to play out. Very often they will increase their practice time because they don't want to be embarrassed and have their stand partners think they are inferior players.

The procedure of placing all the good players near the front can weaken the ensemble. Not only will all the less qualified people be together with no strong players to lead them, but they will be farther away from the director. This can result in ragged ensemble playing since they are not as quick in observing the beat as the better players.

Distribution of Violin Players

The director should place some of his strong players in the second violin section and not concentrate all of them in the firsts. Unless there is good leadership in each section, the group will suffer. One rule I have always observed is that the violinists coming into the high school orchestra from the lower schools spend one year in the second section. This has always been understood by the younger players and there have been no problems. One reason for doing this is to help all the violinists gain an appreciation of the importance of this section, often looked down upon by some people. Another reason is to maintain a rather loose seniority system and to sometimes solve the problem of the advanced young player mentioned a few paragraphs previously. If there happened to be no holdover from the previous year capable of handling the position of principal of the second violins, and a proficient younger player was coming in, I started him out in that position. The students have always known that I rate that position on a par with assistant concertmaster, and there have been occasions when students asked to be considered for it rather than moved into the firsts. Some students never get out of the second section, but they do fine work there and do not feel inferior. Through careful explanations and selection of music in which the seconds have important passages, the director can instill in these players a high sense of responsibility and worth.

Winds

In the winds, the best players should be given the first parts. However, if the ability of two players is very similar, there is no reason why parts cannot be exchanged sometimes. Should the first player be a senior and the second a junior, the latter can play some of the easier first parts to gain advanced experience for the following year in preparation for moving into first chair by virtue of seniority or challenge.

The first chair players in the wind sections should sit next to each other inasmuch as they often play together. It is much easier for them to play in tune if they can hear each other easily. Figure 2-2 and Figure 2-3 illustrate good seating arrangements for winds.

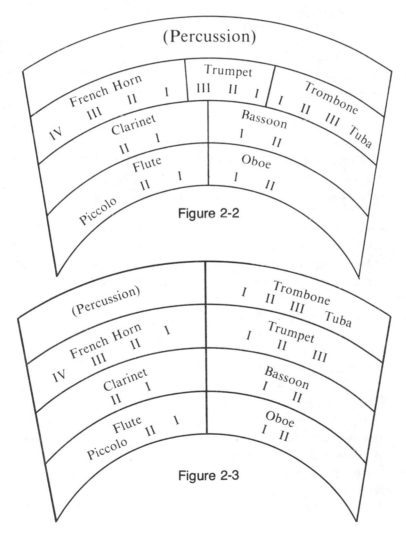

Figure 2-2

Figure 2-3

Other arrangements can be used, depending on the facilities and the personal preference of the director. The important thing is that the first chair people be near each other, either side by side or directly behind each other, if possible.

Percussion

Just a word about the percussion players. I have found it most beneficial to assign the percussionists to learn *all* parts. In case a player should become ill at concert time others are able to cover his parts, at least the most important ones. People enjoy seeing the percussion players switch around; it is part of the visual pleasure for the audience.

HANDLING OF PLACEMENT CHANGES
DURING THE YEAR

Changes in seating will most likely occur during the course of the school year due to many factors. Certain students may advance faster than others, both technically and musically, because of extra and careful practice. Others may fail to progress, or even slip, in effort and accomplishment. They may not have as much time to practice as some others, or may not have the drive. It might be well to move them about, either because of student requests or the decision of the director, unless seniority is adhered to 100%. Sometimes a student may realize that he is more competent than someone sitting ahead of him, but, due to the fact that the latter is a senior, will courteously not request an opportunity to change seats.

If the director wishes, he may discuss with the members of the group at the beginning of the year how they wish placement to be done: to have challenges or to have the director decide. If they choose to leave the seating entirely up to the director, he may make changes as he sees fit during the year. If the decision is to have challenges, certain rules should be set up. A procedure that I have found to be effective, fair, and not too time-consuming is as follows:

1. During the last week of each month, the student or students desiring to challenge notify the director.
2. The student may challenge as many people as he wishes, starting with the one directly ahead of him. This allows the person to move up as far as he is capable of going, and places the burden upon those ahead to defend their right to retain their particular chairs. This is quite a motivation to keep improving. (If a violinist has already spent one year in the second section, he may challenge to go into the firsts, provided that there is room for another player in that section without harm to the balance.)
3. The director selects a composition from which certain passages are to

be used, and tells the students involved the page or pages but not the exact passages. The challenge is held after one week.

4. On the designated day, time is taken out of the rehearsal period for these challenges. Usually this is done following the warm-up period. The challenger plays first, followed by the person directly ahead of him. If the vote is favorable to the challenger, he plays again if he wishes to challenge the next player, and so on.

5. The entire orchestra membership votes. Items to be considered in voting are technique, intonation, rhythm, phrasing, and dynamics. Once again, tone quality is not a deciding factor. It is understood that the director retains the prerogative of altering the vote if he feels there might be personal prejudice or any unfairness in the students' votes.

By having this type of challenge only once a month, (some months there might not be any at all), little rehearsal time is lost.

Chapter 3

How to Plan a Productive
Orchestra Rehearsal

A rehearsal requires as much careful consideration and planning as any other class; therefore it is not uncommon for a music director to write out a "lesson plan" for a rehearsal. While this is almost a necessity for the inexperienced person, even a seasoned director will find it useful to have at his side some notes and reminders of the points to be covered during the rehearsal.

OBJECTIVES: HOW DETAILED
SHOULD THEY BE?

Stress One Objective Each Rehearsal

Whatever they are called, some goals or objectives must be set. How detailed should these be? This depends largely upon the individual; however, each rehearsal should have one specific objective upon which intensive attention is focused. Perhaps it will be phrasing. Or dynamics. Or bowing, intonation, articulation, rhythm, style, etc. True, attention to each of these must be a part of every practice. It is good, however, to concentrate especially on one particular area each time. This will help the players become cognizant of these points as well as realize their importance and pay more attention to them in succeeding rehearsals.

41

Some objectives will, of course, be achieved by the end of the rehearsal, while others are long-range, and will be accomplished the day of performance. Some may even be reached years after being presented, as is the case of growth in music appreciation—one of the greatest rewards of my career has been receiving programs of concerts attended by or participated in by my former students, marked with their perceptive comments. When they tell me that their appreciation of music was greatly enhanced by their orchestra work in high school, I feel very gratified.

Objectives should refer not only to the music itself, but to such things as discipline, interest, attention, courtesy, cooperation and punctuality. An orchestra will achieve a goal only as high as that of its director. A conductor who is content to go along with late starts, inattention and poor attendance, as well as incorrect notes, bowing, phrasing, intonation and articulation, will soon have a mediocre, disorganized ensemble. On the other hand, if he is full of energy, enthusiasm, inspiration and ambition, and keeps striving to achieve those objectives that will make the group proud of its accomplishment, continued growth will be attained.

Make Objectives Known

It is best if the director states what the day's objectives are to the players at the beginning of each rehearsal. True, a rehearsal can be productive if only the *director* knows the objectives he is working toward. However, how much easier to accomplish them if he and the entire ensemble are pulling together! Of course, the students will probably realize what he is striving for, but the rapport will be enriched if he takes them into his confidence.

How many objectives and how detailed to include in a rehearsal will be, in part, dictated by the ability of the players themselves. It is essential, however, that objectives be specific and detailed enough to be meaningful to the students and bring some measure of recognizable achievement during the rehearsal.

FOUR ADVANTAGES OF
A SCHEDULE ON CHALKBOARD

An extremely useful device for having a productive rehearsal is to have the day's schedule on the chalkboard before the students arrive. This should include the particular parts of each selection to be rehearsed if each is not to be done in its entirety. The director's card given on page 93, Chapter 7, is an example of what can be done. The announcements can be included at the bottom of the chalkboard.

Four definite advantages of this system are:

1. The students get in the habit of looking at the board as soon as they

enter the room. They begin thinking about the music right away and get their sheets in the proper order as per the schedule, thus the rehearsal can start promptly. They should put the selections on the right side of the stand so that, as they turn pages, each selection will be face down on the left side when finished. The next selection is then already in place on the right side. A schedule also makes the players aware of about how much time will be spent in each area. The psychology here is that since there is a time limit (while not airtight), as much as possible should be accomplished within that span.

2. Loss of rehearsal time while someone looks for a part is avoided. Nothing is more irritating to a director who is already pressed for time than to have to wait for people to get the right selection from the folder.

3. Loss or misplacement of a part is revealed immediately and there is time to obtain another from the librarian or make arrangements to share with another player.

4. Brief practice of specified passages indicated for special attention during the course of the rehearsal is possible. Short as these warm-ups may be (depending upon how quickly a student gets to orchestra from the previous class and gets ready to play), they do reveal their worth over a period of time.

Before becoming aware of the value of having the daily schedule on the board, rehearsals with my high school orchestra were not utilized to their fullest. The students would enter the rehearsal room, and not knowing the agenda for the day's rehearsal, could not get their music in order. Therefore, much talking took place, some of it *fortissimo!* (Some talking before and after rehearsals is only natural, but it can be kept to a minimum if the students know that they should have their music in order by a specific time and should warm up a bit.)

There was time lost while players looked for their parts after the rehearsal was under way. The opportunity to practice certain difficult passages was lost unless the students took it upon themselves to do this, and they are much more likely to do it if they know which selections are scheduled for that day.

All in all, I estimate that at least 10% rehearsal efficiency was lost before implementing this system.

USING SIGHT-READING EFFECTIVELY

Each rehearsal, except a final one prior to a concert, should contain some sight-reading. How long and extensive this is will be determined by such factors as performance dates, how well music is progressing in preparation for concerts, the type of problems encountered, etc.

Placement of Sight-reading

When to sight-read is important. Some directors prefer to open the rehearsal in such a manner; however, I have found that placing it between two numbers that are being worked out makes for a refreshing change. Also, the work on the previous number where specific objectives are kept in mind will aid in the sight-reading process. This is especially true if the work chosen for sight-reading contains one or more of the details just worked on. The goal here is to see whether or not the players are able to carry over, spot these similarities, and execute the passages with some degree of facility.

Rhythm Is Important

There should always be a purpose in sight-reading. To run through a selection just to be playing at sight is a waste of time. The players should be instructed to do as many things correctly as they can. This includes playing in the right key and also watching the intonation, dynamics and rhythm. I have always placed emphasis upon getting the rhythm as accurate as possible, even if it means leaving out notes in rapid passages or in ones with several accidentals. This will permit the sight-reading to proceed with a minimum of stopping. Since, in many cases, it is the rhythm that gives young players the greatest difficulty, concentrating on this will help improve their rhythmical sense.

Slowing the tempo a bit in sight-reading can be helpful, because sometimes the result of playing a number through at the prescribed tempo might be chaos. Experienced directors know that even high school players will pick up the tempo in sight-reading until the music feels "right" at the expense of rhythm and intonation. This is natural for a musical person and should not be criticized. Attention should be drawn to the fact that this shows a mature development of the young musical mind; *however*, caution should be exercised and a "run-away" situation not permitted. Understanding between director and players will help solve this problem.

Stress the Positive

Taking time to compliment whatever is done well during the sight-reading part of the rehearsal is beneficial. Be specific. Just saying "not bad" is not enough. Telling them, for instance, that between points A and B their rhythm was very good, will help make their day. Also be mindful of their dynamic achievements. If they can, at the first reading, observe some of the dynamics as indicated, they are doing very well. This they should be told. As a rule, I pass over the passages that were rugged. They already know it—why remind them? The purpose of sight-reading is to see how much they can do well, not how much they do badly.

HOW TO MOTIVATE INTEREST
DURING REHEARSALS

One of the greatest pitfalls of any rehearsal is loss of interest. As interest declines, so does achievement, and rehearsal time is so precious that no director can afford to lose even minutes because of failure to maintain interest. How does one keep the interest of the players at a peak? It isn't always easy, but there are little things that can be done to help.

Use Compliments

One of the best ways is to create interest before a single note of any selection is played. This is done simply by taking no more than a minute to say, "Yesterday we (I use the word *'we'* because the orchestra and director always work as a team) did very well on the first part of this. Let's try to do as well from here to the end." It motivates interest in doing something well.

Play for Each Other

Another method is to have one of the sections play a brief passage to show what improvement has been made. The rest of the orchestra becomes the audience. Interest is there because usually the section selected is not known beforehand. Thus, the students give some thought to the possibility that their section might get to "perform." Here is anticipation—something to look forward to. A word of caution: Be reasonably sure that the section chosen will be able to do the passage quite well by listening carefully as the selection is rehearsed.

Sequence Is Important

The order of rehearsing the various selections helps keep up interest. If the rehearsal includes, say, two numbers in moderate tempo, they should not be taken back to back. Better to split them up and do something in a different tempo and style in between.

Vary the Music

Variety is important. Using selections of different lengths, from different periods and in different styles helps create interest. Directors who concentrate the bulk of their offerings in, say, baroque or contemporary, may find interest beginning to lag. It is comparable to a steady diet of ice cream, which, while being very good, eventually loses its appeal because of sameness.

Score Reading and Conducting

An idea used by a colleague, Mr. Normand Poulshock of Sammamish High

School, Bellevue, Washington, is an excellent one for keeping up interest. To teach conducting techniques and score reading, he sometimes shows slides of the conductor's score and everyone conducts. Playing a recording of the selection being studied helps. Students are usually fascinated by the score, and studying it a bit helps them understand something about reading it. It also makes them aware of what the other parts of the orchestra are doing. This may make them listen more to the other sections while playing their own parts, because not listening is always a weakness in young players. This method also cuts down on rehearsal time needed to bring a composition to performance level. (It is understood that only slides of scores that are in the public domain are used in this way so as not to infringe on the copyright law.)

Humor Can Be Helpful

There are times when the director can call upon his own experience in the past regarding something of interest to the students. A passage or a particular work being rehearsed may bring to mind a "goof" he may have made or something that may have happened at a rehearsal or concert.

I recall an incident that could have resulted in confusion and embarrassment. I was about to conduct my orchestra at a contest-festival event, the group having been selected to perform its contest selection on the evening program. The work was *Zampa Overture* by Herold. As I stepped upon the podium, the *Secret Marriage Overture* by Cimarosa ran through my mind for some unknown reason. Up went the baton, up came the instruments, and up came the preparatory beat which, of course, was not the correct tempo for *Zampa*. Fortunately, I caught the error in time, stopped the preparatory beat, then gave the correct tempo. This occurrence made the orchestra members aware that they are not the only ones who, at times, slip up.

Telling such incidents occasionally will appeal to the young people and they will tend to look forward to hearing some of these anecdotes during rehearsals.

Performances

Arrange for several performances each semester. Interest will be created in rehearsals, as each performance will be a goal toward which to work.

SIX SPECIFIC WAYS TO KEEP
A REHEARSAL MOVING

Once the rehearsal has begun, it becomes the duty of the director to keep it moving along. If this is done effectively, the period will be over before the orchestra members are aware of it and they will complain that it went all too fast.

Here are six successful ways in which this can be accomplished:

1. Plan every minute of the period. If the director is well-prepared and

every minute is accounted for, there is no time for delay. The rehearsal can do nothing but move ahead.

2. Do not work with any one section separately for more than two or three minutes. The rest of the players will become inattentive. Talking may take place. Wind instruments can "cool off."

3. Do not always stop the orchestra to mention something that may be amiss. If possible, indicate this by "speaking" loudly over the sound. This saves a "stop and go" situation. This system may be applied to both criticism and praise. Sometimes a nod or facial expression in the direction of the section or individual player will accomplish more than stopping the entire group. In fact, in most cases, I have not stopped the orchestra if an individual player made an error. I merely looked at him, he at me, and we both understood. This accomplished more than stopping and making an issue out of the matter. Sometimes I have asked a section to play a passage over even though one player was in error. I do this only if improvement could not be accomplished with a gesture.

4. If the temperature in the room appears to increase, take immediate steps to cool it down. It probably won't be possible to open the hall door without treating the entire floor to a "concert." If the room has no windows that can be opened, turn the thermostat down if it is possible to do this. (Some schools have "set" thermostats and if this is the case an understanding with the maintenance department about room temperature should be agreed upon.) I have always taken the opportunity to explain a passage or mention any notices the students should hear while the room cools off. In the end, no rehearsal time was lost as rehearsing went on during the normal comment time.

5. Avoid taking time out to talk to someone in the hall. Let it be understood that during the rehearsal there should be no outside interruptions allowed unless there is an emergency of some kind. Stopping a rehearsal to answer the phone or talk about a student's progress can be very disruptive and should not be permitted. I have always encouraged school officials and parents to make appointments for discussions. This works out best for everyone.

6. If possible, stay within the schedule placed on the chalkboard, even if everything hoped for is not accomplished. When it is time to go to the next selection—go. This will lay the burden for not reaching all of the objectives upon the players and should stimulate them to do better the next day. By moving on they will understand that you are determined to keep the rehearsal on schedule. They, too, want to do this. They are looking forward to the closing selection which, as a rule, is one they now play quite well.

If, for some reason (and there could be several), the rehearsing of a specific selection is not going well, it can be dropped and the next one on the agenda started. Sometimes the director can tell that to keep hammering at something when nothing seems to be happening can be futile and cause a loss of interest. On the other hand, there may be the occasional time when things are not going too well but everyone is working hard and the director and students feel that just a bit more work will really pay off. They can agree to skip the final selection and perhaps have a little longer time for a particularly favorite number the next day. The director does have to be a bit flexible at times, and this will enrich his relationship with the group.

DESIGNING THE THREE PARTS
OF A REHEARSAL

Exposition, Development, Coda

A rehearsal can be constructed in much the same manner as a musical composition. For example, a movement of a symphony starts with the exposition, then goes on to the development, and generally has a conclusion which may be considered the climax. Likewise, a rehearsal can be patterned in a similar fashion.

Considering the period as a whole, the exposition would cover passing out music, getting out instruments, putting music in order, private warm-ups, tuning, drill or warm-ups by entire group and running through portions or all of a selection worked on the previous day. All of the above would serve as the first part of the rehearsal.

Next comes the development. This should be considered the heaviest part of the period. Here is where details are worked out and sight-reading may take place. It is by far the most intensive part of the rehearsal, requiring keen and continual concentration.

The ending, or if we want to use the musical term, coda, will consist of playing a rather polished work and include any announcements or comments deemed necessary. Also it allows time for putting away instruments and picking up the music.

A rehearsal so divided will be the most productive. The exposition time helps the players to "get in step" so to speak, allowing them to get their fingers limbered up, wind instruments warmed up and percussionists' arms and wrists relaxed. This will make it possible to accomplish the utmost during the development portion of the period. It is rather a waste of time to begin detailed work before the students are "loosened up" or in the correct frame of mind.

The coda or conclusion may be considered the frosting on the cake. At times

I have referred to this part as the dessert. While still attentive, there is a feeling of relaxation in playing something that has been worked over for some time. Now the fruit of their labor has blossomed. Music should be relaxing at times; here is that opportunity.

The director will see, at once, that the time should not be divided into three equal parts. It becomes obvious that the middle portion should be the longest. The approximate mathematical division that I have found most suitable is 1/4, 1/2, 1/4. This gives the in-depth work about one-half of the rehearsal.

There are times when, due to circumstances beyond the control of the director, a period is shortened or the arrangement is not feasible. Then he has to decide what should be eliminated. A good rule to follow is to keep as much of the development section as possible in the rehearsal. This can be done by cutting back on both the first and last parts. It will do no harm to reduce the warm-up period and not play as much of the last selection. When confronted with this situation, I would use only the last portion of the final number which would still bring the rehearsal to a climax as planned. To leave a composition that is near performance level, in the middle, tends to destroy the musical mood. That is hardly a good way to end a rehearsal. The psychology the director was required to take in college comes in handy in situations such as these.

Generally, adherence to the three parts of a rehearsal will insure maximum efficiency and benefit from the time invested by all.

Chapter 4

The Non-Musical Aspects of Rehearsals and How to Handle Them

The physical aspects of a rehearsal site affect the players in many important ways. We all want our rehearsals to be as musically fruitful as possible, and the non-musical points in this chapter will help achieve this goal. Many music directors find their surroundings to be below ideal standards, but work can be done to improve rehearsal facilities as well as places of performance. This is a continuing process.

Not a great deal can be done about rooms and auditoriums once they are built, but sometimes acoustics and sound isolation can be improved by adding curtains, drapes, etc., or by purchasing or constructing an acoustical shell. Storage cabinets can be built or purchased,and sometimes arrangements can be made for better lighting, ventilation, etc.*

---

*It is impossible to include everything here, but a very good reference book is *Music Buildings, Rooms and Equipment*, edited by Charles L. Gary and published by Music Educators National Conference, Reston, Virginia (formerly Washington, D.C.) in 1966. This book is now out of print, but there are still many copies available in music libraries. A new book to replace this one has been published in 1975 by Music Educators National Conference: *Planning and Equipping Educational Music Facilities*, edited by Harold Geerdes.

HELP IN PLANNING

If you find yourself in the position of being ''in'' on the designing of new facilities, you can make many suggestions for obtaining the best possible results. I was fortunate in being asked to assist in planning the music facilities for a junior high school in Longview, Washington. The music wing is built at one end of the Monticello Junior High School, with its own outside entrance. This entrance is the nearest point in the school to the adjacent R. A. Long High School, and the facilities were planned to serve both schools.

The administrators requested that the three directors (band, choral, and orchestral) give suggestions and/or drawings of what they would like. My own preference was based upon the design of a radio broadcasting studio I had visited. I realized that the acoustics were very good as I listened to the broadcast of a string ensemble.

Figure 4-1 and Figure 4-2 show that this room is not the customary square room with straight walls. The curves at the rear of the room are the secret to the good acoustics enjoyed in this room. The ceiling was also designed with sound in

Photo by Stuart Fresk

Used by permission of the Longview School District, Longview, Washington

Figure 4-1

Figure 4-2

mind. It is 16 feet in height, which is within the limits of the 14-18 feet recommended for effective acoustics.

Risers are the permanent type and are wide enough to accommodate choral and orchestral rehearsals if necessary. At various times combined rehearsals are held in this room and the orchestra is moved downward, allowing room behind it for the chorus. The top riser is wider than the others, which makes it convenient for the large bass instruments and percussion.

Space is provided at the rear of the room for storage of large instruments such as cellos. A specific area is reserved for the string basses in the hallway between the orchestra and band rooms (see Figure 4-3).

There are two practice rooms adjacent to the main room, and the hallway to the outside is also utilized for practice purposes at times. Upstairs there is one large practice room suitable for up to twelve or so players (depending on the sizes of the instruments), two smaller rooms, storage space, and a room that can be used for instrument repair. The band and choral rooms also have two practice rooms adjacent to the main rooms. The upstairs practice rooms are shared by the three organizations.

Orchestra Room, Monticello Junior High School, Longview, Washington
(Also serves R.A. Long High School)

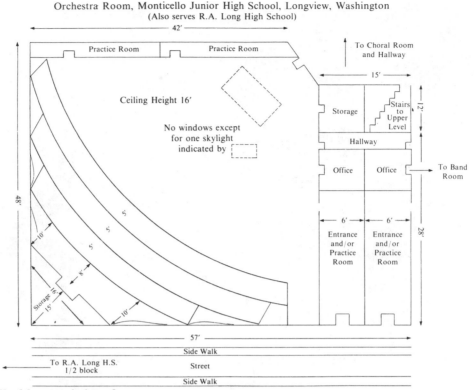

Used by permission of
Longview Public Schools

Figure 4-3

CHECKING OVER REHEARSAL SITE

The rehearsal site should be checked out a few weeks before the opening of school, if at all possible. If you are new to the school system, this is a must. It may seem to be a waste of time if you have worked in the same place for several years and know every square foot of the rehearsal area; however, many odd things can happen during the summer.

I have found, on more than one occasion, that the chairs had been removed during vacation and others put in their place. They were the usual folding chairs most unsuitable for orchestra players. Needless to say, the original ones were promptly returned. At another time, the desk was removed and replaced with a different one. Regular classroom teachers are usually required to have everything out of desk drawers in case any changes are made, but I had thought that the desk in that office was there to stay. Not so, and I had to spend time tracking it down.

Some music rooms have portable chalkboards. If this is the case, these boards are sometimes moved elsewhere during the summer and not returned. I have found it best to request before school is out in the spring that *nothing* be moved out of the orchestra rehearsal room; nevertheless, a survey of the facilities is a good way to save time and be ready for an efficient start on the first day. There are enough details complicating the picture the first few days; you shouldn't have to worry about chairs, chalkboards, etc.

HEATING AND VENTILATION

The matter of ventilation and heat in music rooms must not be overlooked. Oxygen is used and carbon dioxide increases rapidly in a room full of people producing music because of increased inhalation and exhalation of air. If there are no windows, adequate ventilation must be made possible through proper vents, fans, or air conditioning.

Temperature

The ideal temperature of the rehearsal room is around 68 degrees. Maintenance people are not always aware of the fact that an instrumental group in rehearsal tends to generate heat through muscular activity, and this can raise the temperature a few degrees. A room temperature set at 70 or above will affect the mental response of the players as well as the pitch of the instruments. The strings stretch and become flat while the winds go up in pitch. This problem becomes even more acute if a piano is used (especially if it is not up to pitch). It may be impossible to bring the winds down to the piano pitch, resulting in a poor rehearsal. It is your duty to stipulate, quite emphatically if necessary, just what the temperature of your rehearsal room *must* be.

Auditoriums also need to be checked. Many times the stage area where the performers are located becomes almost unbearably hot in order for the audience to be comfortable. This should be investigated before concert time, and perhaps fans can be installed if they are not too noisy or drafty.

> In changing the air within the auditorium, the change must balance the air changes in the stage areas so that the curtains on the stage do not billow. Musicians in the orchestra pit must be provided with adequate ventilation and yet slight drafts on instruments can throw them completely out of tune.[1]

Humidity

Humidity control, something not always considered, is important for musical facilities. This is especially true in any area where above-average humidity occurs with any degree of regularity.

If humidity changes are not controlled, string instruments not only become

---

[1]Charles L. Gary, ed., *Music Buildings, Rooms and Equipment* (Reston, Va. formerly Washington, D.C.; Music Educators National Conference, 1966), p. 77. (See footnote, page 51)

difficult to keep in tune, but can come unglued and will need expert repair to return them to their original playing capacity. Humid atmosphere can affect pianos also, as well as percussion instruments; therefore, precautions should be taken to insure that humidity is not allowed to become excessive where string and percussion instruments are stored. Below are five things that may be done to help this situation:

1. There are dehumidifiers available that can be put in the storage area.

2. Electric light globes (even as low as 25 watts) can be put in the storage cabinets and left on at night, on weekends, and during vacations.

3. Instruments can be moved to another area for an extended time such as during vacation. This can be a room where an electric heater is available and which can be locked for security. (Remember that the instruments should not be too close to the heater as excessive heat will damage them also.)

4. If it is possible to have heat in the music complex without having it on in the entire building, you can request that this be done at times when the humidity is high.

5. Keep pianos away from outside walls.

Air Conditioning

Many schools are now being constructed with air conditioning included, and with few windows. This does help solve some of the problems, especially in some geographical locations and in situations in which the buildings are utilized during most of the year. Unfortunately, a new problem may be created, namely noise. In the music rooms, a constant hum from the air conditioning can be very distracting during a rehearsal. There are ways in which this noise can be reduced to a minimum without impairing the efficiency of the system, and these should be recommended, especially for the music instruction area.

> The first cost of proper heating, air conditioning equipment, and temperature control is small when compared to the benefits to be derived from a comfortable, invigorating environment for music education and from the savings to be effected by minimizing the deterioration of valuable musical instruments.[2]

At times we have all heard comments after a performance to the effect that ''they spoiled the mood of the concert by having to tune so often.'' Perhaps these people can be enlisted to help plan for better ventilation, heating, and cooling systems, or at least to promote such for future buildings.

---

[2]Gary, *Music Buildings, Rooms and Equipment*, p. 78.

HOW TO ACHIEVE PROPER LIGHTING

Poor illumination can very easily cause extra work and fatigue on the part of the group and conductor, whereas adequate lighting can affect mental attitude, enthusiasm, posture, and actual output of energy in a positive way.

Reading music puts somewhat of a strain on the eyes, and the necessity of looking from the music to you (back and forth) while playing can really create a problem if there is not enough light or if there is glare.

The instrument played may be a factor in the lighting problem also. A clarinet or oboe player can sit closer to the music than a trombone player. If the light is bad, the woodwind player may get by, but the trombonist may have difficulty. In the string section, two players share a stand (except for bass players who should each have one). They need to sit somewhat at an angle for bowing and to see the music, and visibility may vary between the two players. Sometimes glare bouncing off a brass instrument can cause visual problems elsewhere in the orchestra.

There is something to be said for the windowless rehearsal room, provided that the artificial lighting is adequate. Problems such as more light in one area than another and too much glare or reflected light are eliminated. Often these rooms are used at night so should be well-lighted by artificial means anyway.

Light Fixture Maintenance

Usually lights are replaced whenever they "burn out." What may not be realized is that the lights may have become rather inefficient before that time, and the lighting in a given room may not be what it should be.

> Particular attention should be given to adequate maintenance of the lighting system. Without a planned program of periodic fixture cleaning and replacement of lamps, illumination levels can drop to half of the installed values in a few months. . . . . Lamp life can be predicted accurately and a relamping and cleaning program for the school should be planned for vacation periods at intervals which approach the useful life of the lamps. . . . .
>
> Care should always be taken to relamp fluorescent fixtures with the proper color of lamps also. Illumination levels as well as colors of walls are greatly affected by the choice of fluorescent lamp color.[3]

How to Select the Right Colors

It is not unusual for the rehearsal room to be repainted during vacation. No one will quarrel with this; however, the color used can be of concern to you. While it is rarely done, a conference with the supervisor of buildings can

---

[3]Gary, *Music Buildings, Rooms and Equipment*, p. 82.

sometimes be of help if he realizes the problems, i.e., that the color used might have a bearing on the amount of light available or cause too much or too little reflected light.

> More and more, educators and school authorities all over the country have become aware of the important part color plays as an aid in creating an atmosphere that promotes efficiency and morale among pupils and teachers alike.[4]

Whether or not a room has windows will make a difference in the choice of colors and placement of them (sometimes more than one color is used in a room, giving it more interest). If there is intense light from windows, a dark color is sometimes used on the opposite wall to help counteract the reflected glare, but, for the most part, the lighter, soft pastels, beige, and cream colors are preferable. Various light shades of the greens and blues seem to be quite popular.

The paint should be flat to cut down on reflected light. On the ceilings, however, reflection is necessary to direct the light downward.

> This restricts the range to white, soft white, cream, ivory, or a very pale tint of a wall color, or a contrasting tint. Such colors should have reflection factors within the range of 80 percent to 85 percent.[5]

The color of the wall that the students face should be easy on the eyes. Also, there should not be too much contrast between the color of the chalkboard and the wall. Many schools are now using the softer green chalkboards rather than the traditional black. I have found that a beige wall, green chalkboard, and yellow chalk seem to produce the least strain on the eyes.

Something not always considered is the color of the floor; when reading music the floor is also in the player's field of vision.

> High level of illumination on the white printed page gives marked contrast against the background of a dark-colored floor. Flooring materials such as tile and carpeting in lighter colors should be used.[6]

RISERS—YES OR NO?

Risers are not a necessity for instrumental groups, but it is easier for the players to see the conductor if they are used. Many schools now have built-in risers in rehearsal rooms, and if the group is accustomed to rehearsing on them, they should also be available wherever concerts are given, if possible. (Collapsible risers are used by some school districts, permitting flexibility in use of the

---

[4]Gary, *Music Buildings, Rooms and Equipment*, p. 83.
[5]Gary, *Music Buildings, Rooms and Equipment*, p. 85.
[6]Gary, *Music Buildings, Rooms and Equipment*, p. 81.

room if different types of activities are carried on there.) If not, seating must be arranged so that every player can see you and vice versa. Players should have music stands at a height that will enable them to see over the tops. There is much going on between the eyes of the performers and conductor, since only two media of communication are available during a performance. Both of these, facial expression and gestures, must take the place of speaking that can be used only at rehearsals. The matter of ''communication'' between players and conductor has many facets and is of vital importance, but the first requirement to good communication is that they can literally see one another.

SELECTION OF CHAIRS

The type of chair used for seating is a very important part of any physical setup for rehearsing. An uncomfortable chair will tire a player quickly. The much-used folding chair should be strictly avoided. These seats usually dip up and then down, causing the occupants to sink back in the chair. One cannot perform well in this position; every musician should sit up straight and not lean against the back of his chair. In order to help this situation, straight-seated as well as straight-backed chairs are needed.

If the only chairs available are not entirely straight-seated, special ones should be obtained for the cello players. Since they must sit on the front half of the chair, a level seat is absolutely essential. (Don't give up trying to get appropriate chairs for everyone.)

For the string bass players I have always provided stools. Since the average player sits somewhat on the edge, padded stools afford more comfort than unpadded ones. They should be 28″ to 30″ high.

Since chairs are being moved about constantly, they should be as light-weight as possible. Also, tabs should be put on each leg. I prefer the small metal ones since they slide easily; rubber tabs tend to break rather quickly, and it becomes necessary to lift the chair each time it is moved.

Whether or not to have chairs with shelves for books underneath is a matter of personal preference. Such a shelf adds a bit of weight and may make the chair more unwieldy to move around, but it does eliminate some of the clutter.

MUSIC STANDS

Many directors, myself included, have had to struggle with metal music stands made in school shops. These are usually quite heavy, and transporting them becomes a chore for students and director alike. Fortunately, the situation has changed in most places; directors today can usually decide on and purchase telescopic metal stands from several good types available. These are much easier to move about.

It is better to have a few extras than not enough. Never should more than two players share a stand (each wind player and percussionist should have his own). I have always had enough stands for the full orchestra, plus at least one for each practice room and several for the large ensemble room. Students should not have to hunt for a stand in order to practice.

If the budget does not provide for the purchase of sufficient stands, there are a couple of alternatives possible:

1. Have some students bring folding stands from home. If they have extras, they can leave one at school; students can alternate in bringing them, but will probably have to be reminded when it is their turn.
2. The orchestra members can arrange projects to raise money to purchase some of the stands. Such things as car washes, paper drives, candy sales, spaghetti dinners, and raffles are some possibilities.

Identification Necessary

Stands should be marked for identification in case they have to be pooled for a performance; then there will be no question as to where each belongs. A stencil can be made from cardboard and spray paint used. The school initials (or name, if short) can be put on, and band and orchestra stands painted different colors if they have separate sets. They can also be numbered, if desired; this is a good way to be sure you get all of them back when they are moved out for a performance. Students can be enlisted to assist with this project. I always put the identification markings on the side of the stand facing the player; in this way they are covered by the music and not noticed by the audience.

THE PODIUM

Some directors choose to use a podium, others do not. If you are especially tall, it may not be needed. If risers are used, the necessity for one is lessened also.

A podium, under the average conditions, facilitates each player seeing you and vice versa, thus giving each confidence in the other. Also, it helps to discipline in a quiet way, because all eyes are focused on the person standing "up in front" of the group.

The podium should be large enough to hold, with room to spare, a rehearsal swivel chair, if you care to sit briefly at intervals in the rehearsal. My preference in podium size is 4' x 4' x 8" high. To avoid the possibility of a mishap, an edge ½" to ¾" high should be put on the back side.

The podium can be left unpainted, or painted so that shoe marks are not too visible. My preference is to paint the sides and cover the top with indoor-outdoor carpeting of a conservative color and pattern. It is best to avoid a loud or flashy color that would tend to draw attention to the conductor and away from the orchestra.

Slots put in two opposite sides of the podium will be helpful in moving it.

ADEQUATE INSTRUMENT
STORAGE SPACE NECESSARY

Some type of storage space for instruments in or near rehearsal rooms is essential. Ideally, most of this should be adjoining the room rather than in it, as there is less confusion at the beginning and end of the rehearsal period. There are many arrangements: shelves can be provided for small instruments and compartments for larger ones, or all compartments can be made. With thefts of instruments on the increase, it seems necessary these days to have doors that can be locked on the storage room or cabinets. Smaller instruments can be kept in students' lockers if necessary; obviously this is impossible with larger ones, and if they are left lying about, damage can easily occur. A cabinet to hold the many small percussion instruments is very convenient. (See Figure 4-4.)

**Used by permission of Norren Manufacturing Inc.,
Azusa, California**

Figure 4-4

If you find yourself in a situation where there is no provision for storage, effort should be directed toward getting some compartments built in. Since the school district usually supplies the large instruments as well as the percussion equipment, it should not be difficult to convince the administrators that adequate storage facilities are necessary to protect their investments. If you are consulted in the planning of a music wing of a new building, remember to include this important part of the structure in your suggestions.

STEEL FILES VS.
SHELVES FOR MUSIC LIBRARY

Ample space should be provided for storage of the music. If a separate room is not available, a reasonable alternative is to use a portion of one or more practice rooms, provided that they are large enough. It is also possible to store music along the walls of the rehearsal room if there is no other place.

Which is better, steel files or wooden shelves? I have used both, but settled on the shelves for the following reasons:

1. It seems quicker to locate a selection on a shelf than in a drawer. Everything is right there in plain sight.
2. Taking music off a shelf seems easier than pulling it out of a drawer, especially a top drawer.
3. It is not as difficult to move the music around as the library grows.
4. It is less expensive to build shelves than to purchase steel files.

The only disadvantage I see in the shelves is that the music can get a bit dusty. Some directors wish to keep all music under lock and key; this is a matter of personal preference. I have never felt that there was any necessity for locking it up. Whichever method is used, alphabetical dividers are necessary for quick location of selections.

A MUSIC SORTING RACK CAN BE HELPFUL

A music sorting rack is very handy for use when the music is put in the folders and again when it is taken out and filed away for future use. (See Figure 4-5.)

**Used by permission of Norren Manufacturing Inc.,
Azusa, California**

Figure 4-5

MUSIC CABINET FOR INDIVIDUAL FOLDERS

A music storage cabinet with slots for each individual folder is very useful. With each slot marked for identification, i.e., 1st Violin, Stand I; 1st Flute; 2nd Trumpet, etc., there is little likelihood that a student will come in after school and take the wrong part home for practice. Also, it is possible to see at a glance which folders are out or have not been replaced after rehearsal. (See Figure 4-6.)

Photo by John Diehnel

Figure 4-6

CHALKBOARDS

You should remember that you, as a music director, are not only a conductor but also a teacher. Chalkboards are very essential for your work.

I like to have two boards, one built in and the other movable on wheels because there are times when it is beneficial to move a board closer to the group or put it at a different angle so that all may see it clearly.

Having permanent staff lines on at least part of one board is a good idea. No clefs should be on the lines, since different clefs are used by orchestra players. (Not having to draw lines with a staff liner saves time. I have found that often when I had to use a liner, a piece or two of chalk might be missing. Time was wasted looking for chalk, inserting it, and then drawing the lines.) Ample chalk should be available in all chalkboard trays at all times. A student can have the assignment of checking at the beginning of the rehearsal each day to see that there is plenty in place.

Written material on a staffed chalkboard is difficult for the students to read, especially for those at a distance from it. Therefore, it makes sense to leave one board blank for listing the rehearsal schedule, general instructions and information, illustrating certain problems and solutions, and for use by other classes should they be assigned to the same room.

COAT RACKS

Depending on the geographical location of the school, a coat rack may be a useful and courteous item to have available. If the music department is in a separate area and must be reached by going outside of the main building, there must be a place for wraps. At the very least, coat hooks should be provided somewhere. Coats should not be put on the backs of chairs nor on the floor. They can be an accident hazard, as people (including directors) can trip on them while walking around the room.

AVAILABILITY OF PRACTICE ROOMS

Practice rooms are a facility peculiar to the teaching of music with some special problems not encountered by administrators or architects in planning other elements of the school. Among the factors which must be considered are isolation of sound, size, ventilation, amount of use, and supervision.[7]

Practice rooms fulfill a very definite need. Students who play the large instruments such as tuba and string base can practice before or after school.

---

[7]Gary, *Music Buildings, Rooms and Equipment*, p. 31.

Individuals or small groups can work out difficult passages in practice rooms while a sectional rehearsal is going on in the main room.

The size of the practice rooms depends largely on the total square footage available for the entire music facility. Some of them can be quite small for individual practice, but it is a good idea to have some large enough to accommodate ensembles. Thus more than one ensemble can work simultaneously. Some of the rooms should have pianos in them, and all should have some type of window in the door for the purpose of supervision.

MISCELLANEOUS

In addition to those mentioned throughout this chapter, the following items are appropriate and convenient for the music department to have:

1. Bulletin boards for notices, articles of interest, program write-ups, musical cartoons, etc.
2. Showcases in which to display awards, pictures, etc.
3. Drinking fountain. This is a real help, especially for wind players. It is then unnecessary for students to go into the hall for a drink. This eliminates the distraction of opening and closing the rehearsal room door.
4. Telephone. It is a great convenience to have a telephone in a music building or complex so that students can call for rides home when they return at night from concerts, contests, festivals, etc. Also, if the rooms are used for community group rehearsals, those involved appreciate having a phone available.
5. Some type of end pin holders for use by cellists. These not only protect the floor, but keep the instrument from slipping. I have always utilized ''T-Squares'' which can be made in the school shop. These are made from two pieces of ¾" thick wood. (See Figure 4-7.) Half of the wood

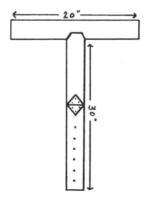

Figure 4-7

is cut out of each piece where they are to be joined, and they are fitted together and nailed. The pieces are approximately 1⅜" wide. The top of the "T" fits behind the front legs of the chair to hold it in place. Holes are drilled part of the way through the wood in the other piece. Usually they are 2" apart, but can be closer if it is more convenient for the player. If desired, a hinge can be put in this piece, making it more compact and easier to carry about.

Some of the foregoing may seem to be insignificant details, but in the long run they help make successful, well-organized rehearsals. If all participants are comfortable physically, their mental and emotional attitudes are more favorable toward working and learning.

Chapter 5

Key Musical Preparations
for the First Rehearsal

The first rehearsal will be only as good as the preparation for it. Whatever can be done ahead of time must be done. (For example, tryouts for new people should be held prior to the opening of school.) Why take valuable rehearsal time for things that can be taken care of beforehand? The first rehearsal should consist mostly of playing, not talking, sorting and/or stamping or fingering music. A smashing first rehearsal, even though the group may sound *somewhat* under par, will instill a feeling of anticipation of more such well-organized rehearsals during the rest of the year. In reality, the very first rehearsal is a sales pitch —the director is "selling" himself to the orchestra members through organization, foresight and adequate planning. It won't take the students long to realize that their director is well-prepared and ready to "go." This will get the orchestra off to a very satisfying start.

Some of the matters discussed in this chapter are things to think about at other times as well as just at the beginning of the year. The sections regarding the repertoire and using arrangements would fall into this category.

INVENTORY OF ORCHESTRA MUSIC
AVAILABLE IN LIBRARY

Long before school opens, a thorough inventory of what music is available should be taken. The director who has been in the same school for a number of years will know what he has and will already have ordered music in the spring for the following year or at least for the first part of the year. The new director should become acquainted with the library and decide whether or not he wishes to order any new music. He should also find out from the administration what funds are available for his department so he knows exactly how to budget his money.

If no written inventory of music is on hand, one should be made. Sometimes student help is available for tasks such as this, and if it can't be done before school opens, it should be taken care of as soon as possible. I have found that 3×5 cards (ruled) filed alphabetically by composition work very well. It is hardly necessary to crossfile by composer. When looking for a certain selection, it is quicker to find it under the title than to look through the various selections by a composer. (Sometimes I find that I remember a title but not the composer, especially if it is a short number and the composer not well-known.)

The file will also serve a useful purpose if a record of missing parts is kept. This will enable the librarian or the director to check quickly and see if any parts should be ordered. Figure 5-1 shows how the card might look:

Title: Zampa Overture
Composer: Herold
Publisher:
Instrumentation: A Ⓑ C   Symphonic
Parts Missing
Inst.   Replaced   Inst. Replaced
Trumpet II   5/10/   Tuba (on order)
Viola IV

Figure 5-1

The reverse side of the card may be used as well for continuation of parts missing. Notations regarding these parts can be made in pencil and erased when replaced, or crossed off, if desired. However, the person in charge of this particular duty should always be sure to make the notations so that the file is up-to-date and accurate.

Any selections in the library that are not stamped with the name of the high school should be so marked, and all parts numbered in sequence. This allows for easy assembling when parts are turned in and music is put back in the file.

INVENTORY OF MUSICAL INSTRUMENTS
OWNED BY SCHOOL

The next step is to know what instruments are school-owned. Again, a new director will need to obtain this information. Others will merely have to check to see which instruments have been loaned out during the summer and to whom. If a director moves to a new location, he should leave a list of the school instruments and to whom any have been checked out for the summer.

Again, an easy way of keeping records is with cards. A 4×6 card is a good size for the instrument card file, and these can be lined or unlined as desired. They can be duplicated and a supply kept on hand. Figure 5-2 and Figure 5-3 are samples of both sides of such a card.

```
┌─────────────────────────────────────────────────────────────┐
│                 Instrumental Music Department                 │
│                                                               │
│        _____ School      │
│                                                               │
│  Instrument _____ Make _____        │
│                                                               │
│  Where Purchased _____ Cost _____        │
│                                                               │
│  When Purchased _____ Serial # _____        │
│                                                               │
│  Condition _____         │
│                                                               │
│  Case _____ Bow _____ Rosin _____ Mute _____ Key _____ │
│                                                               │
│  Mouthpiece _____ Crooks _____ Lyre _____ Strap _____ │
│                                                               │
│  Oil _____ Swab _____                                     │
│                                                               │
│  Comments:                                                    │
└─────────────────────────────────────────────────────────────┘
```

Figure 5-2

Name _____ Phone _____

Address _____

Out Date_____ In Date _____ Condition _____

Name _____ Phone _____

Address _____

Out Date _____ In Date_____ Condition _____

Name _____ Phone _____

Address _____

Out Date_____ In Date _____ Condition _____

Figure 5-3—Reverse Side

These school-owned instruments should be checked carefully to be sure that they are in top condition and that any repairs ordered in the spring have been carried out. Frustration on the part of a player during the first rehearsal because valves are stuck or strings are broken is hardly conducive to a pleasant beginning. Any student who has checked an instrument out for the summer should be responsible for any repairs due to his carelessness. This should be understood ahead of time.

You should have a supply of strings, rosin, tuners, tail-guts, mutes, and valve oil for school-owned instruments. Also, arrangements should be made to have the school pianos tuned before school starts. In some cases the music supervisor takes care of this, but it should not be overlooked.

WHAT CONSTITUTES
A GOOD MUSIC REPERTOIRE?

Variety

A repertoire must include music from all periods and cover the many various styles. To concentrate on only one or two types of music can deprive the student of one of the basic reasons for being in the orchestra: learning. Also, this can soon cause loss of interest. The orchestra affords a fine opportunity for students to be constantly exposed to different kinds of music.

Challenging Works

The repertoire should also contain music that probably will not be presented at any performance, simply because it is too difficult. Nevertheless, students should be given an opportunity to take a crack at some of this material. Reading through some difficult works and "getting their teeth into them," may get players interested in listening to recordings or tapes by professional orchestras, and may also challenge them to work harder so that they may be able to execute more difficult material in college or later in life.

Light Music

A number of easy, tuneful, pleasant selections, "novelty" numbers and some of the popular music of the day should also be on hand. These will provide a refreshing change for the students and will also come in handy when the orchestra is called upon, sometimes on short notice, to fill in with some 15-20 minutes of music for a gathering where heavier works might not be suitable, e.g. playing a short program at some type of community gathering or before and between acts of a school play. This type of music should be perused carefully before purchasing to be sure it is in a good orchestral style.

String Music

Basically, about half of an orchestra library should contain music for strings alone. There is an abundance of string literature available at all levels to suit any high school string section. Some of the finest works are for strings, and compositions of each era in the development of music should be explored.

A good music repertoire contains balanced material suitable for educational purposes as well as for performance. The director should never lose sight of the basic reasons for the school orchestra: exposing the student to as much rich orchestral literature as possible; teaching him how to play it in the correct style; and, furthering his interest in music to the utmost.

WHAT ARE THE MUSICAL VALUES OF USING ARRANGEMENTS?

If the music library of the average high school orchestra contained only the original music written for the standard symphony orchestra, there would be much which would be unplayable by the group. Not only is much of it far too difficult, but the instrumentation called for is often beyond the realm of the average high school orchestra. There are, therefore, musical values to the use of arrangements. Below are seven justifications for using good arrangements:

1. It is possible for the orchestra to explore and perform much of the fine musical literature that would be too difficult in the original form.
2. The instrumentation will generally be suitable for high school orchestra and will contain adequate cross-cues and ad lib parts.
3. In most cases the parts have been marked with bowings and fingerings in the strings, and alternate fingerings are often indicated for winds. Complicated rhythms such as $\frac{7}{4}$ are divided into 4 and 3 or 3 and 4, with a ¦ to indicate the division. The higher positions of the first violins are often eliminated or are divided to allow the less advanced players to play the lower notes.
4. Often these arrangements are somewhat less expensive than the original.
5. It is possible to purchase only one or two movements of a symphony.
6. Often the music itself is in a larger print than the original, making it easier to read.
7. Nearly always the orchestration will include an introduction pointing out general and often specific items that the director may wish to give attention to. If the music is of a programmatic nature, a paragraph or two telling what the composer had in mind is often given. This can be an aid in understanding the music itself. Many times such a foreword will appear on each individual part which allows each student to read it also.

Try to use as many original works as the group is able to play. This may mean some detailed analysis of the works by the great composers so that the director can decide which will fit into the capabilities of his orchestra.

When looking over arrangements, the director must check carefully lest he find that some of the scores he selects are somewhat below the standard he wishes to maintain.

12 Point Checklist for Judging Arrangements

Unfortunately, all arrangements are not well done. What should the director look for in such modified works?

1. Did the arranger keep as close as possible to the original instrumentation?
2. Is the style preserved such as bowing, slurs, staccato, phrasing, etc.?
3. Are dynamics clearly marked?
4. Are cross-cues adequate and wisely chosen?
5. Are there too many cuts, thus destroying the sense of structure?

6. Have some parts been made far too easy?
7. Are French horns and trumpets in F or B^b or A rather than in their original keys? (This is an aid to these players; however, they should eventually learn to transpose from the original without rewriting the part if they intend to play much serious music.)
8. Are extra brass parts added just for weight?
9. Are unnecessary percussion parts added?
10. Does the arrangement contain a full conductor's score?
11. Does the composition really lend itself to arranging from the original?
12. Will the arrangement be an adequate educational substitute for the original?

WAYS TO ENLARGE REPERTOIRE
WITHOUT MUCH COST
OR COPYRIGHT LAW INFRINGEMENT

In these days (when were they ever different?) getting money for orchestral music is not always an easy matter, and enlarging the music library becomes difficult. The director who gives up on collecting new material and pulls out old stuff time after time is letting his orchestra down. It is true that about every 3-4 years one can start going through the library again, since the students have changed. However, there should be ways to explore new selections periodically in order to expand the musical horizons of the players. Just how this can be done on a limited budget will be discussed here.

If there is only one high school in a system, the director may be more fortunate than some of his neighbors in larger systems. There may be more money available for just the one school, although this is not always the case. If not, what is the director to do? Following are suggestions that some of my colleagues and I have found to be very workable:

1. Contact an orchestra director in a nearby high school.
    a) Suggest that you swap selections from time to time.
    b) When ordering new music, have a conference and each order different selections.
    c) Make a typewritten copy of what is available and send one to the other director; he does the same.
    d) Get together in early fall and decide tentatively which selections each plans to use from his own library, and then the others can be available on a loan basis.
    e) Make clear to all parties that any parts lost will be replaced by the borrower. A checklist should be included with each selection loaned out, and checked over upon the return of the music. The librarian or other student helper can be enlisted to take care of the paper work.

2. If there is a college or university nearby, music may sometimes be borrowed from the orchestral library there.

3. On certain occasions it might be feasible to rent, from the publisher, a work or two that might be too expensive to buy, but which would be useful to the group. If rented for two months the piece could be presented at a performance.

4. Visit the local music store (or one in the nearest large city) and ask if they have any orchestral music that is not moving. If it turns out to be something that can be effectively used, sometimes a deal can be made to take this off their inventory for a somewhat reduced price. Music collecting dust on the shelves of a store does not help pay expenses. If some of the music desired is out of print permanently and it has one or more parts missing from it, it is perfectly permissible (under certain circumstances) to copy the parts needed from the score. A check should be made with the publisher for copyright purposes and also inquiry made to see if, by chance, the publisher might be able to supply copies of individual parts on a special order.

5. The public libraries of some large cities have orchestral music that may be borrowed.

In a city with two or more high schools, the same idea of exchanging music and building up libraries of different selections works very well. In some large cities there is a central library only, and each director checks out his selections there. This works out well if the music supervisor asks the directors to request music they would like and the library is enlarged and enriched from time to time.

THE CONTENTS OF THE DIRECTOR'S FOLDER

His folder is as important to the director as a tool box is to the electrician. It should contain *everything* that he might need during the rehearsal. The players should not be made to wait while the director runs to his office to pick up something that should have been in the folder. For the director to have everything at his immediate disposal does wonders for the morale of the group. When the students see how well-organized the director is at the very first rehearsal, they will be willing to consider him an efficient teacher.

Just what should be in the director's folder?

1. All the scores for music to be used at the rehearsal.

2. Two pencils with erasers, one black and at least one colored. There will be times when the director wishes to change something, and it should be marked at that moment. To rely upon memory and doing it later is a poor practice. Since some directors use different colored pencils for different items such as tempo, phrasing, repeat marks, key

changes, etc., it is essential that one of each color is available in the folder.

3. A roster listing the names of the players, addresses, phone numbers, and instruments played. It is also advisable to have listed the year in school of each player. This will tell the director at a glance how long he can expect each one to be with him. It will serve as a basis for planning replacements. Some directors prefer to have all this information in the grade book. My preference is to have both—the roster in the folder and the grade book to carry around.

4. A small screwdriver and small thin-nosed pliers for emergency use for wind instruments. Also some string for the French horn players for their valves. My own experience has been that few, if any, wind players are prepared in such a way. (Before the semester is over, the players themselves should have these items at their disposal.)

5. One extra baton (if a baton is used). Directors (including myself) will many times use the baton to beat upon the stand to emphasize a difficult rhythmical pattern. Sooner or later pieces break off and the baton gets smaller and smaller and becomes useless. There are also times when a baton will simply fly out of the director's hand and sail into the orchestra! How easy to just pick up the spare and go right on!

6. Several pieces of manuscript paper without clefs. They can be dittoed sheets. There are times when a player may wish to write out a phrase or several lines for one reason or another, or the director may wish to write something out for a player. Usually this is done just before the period begins or at the end of it, so as not to take up rehearsal time. It is very handy to have the paper right there and not have to go to the office and look through drawers to get it.

7. Fingernail file, preferably a long one. Often string players will play out of tune because of lengthy fingernails on the left hand. Few carry nail files with them, so the director can suggest they use the one in his folder if they forgot to file their nails at home.

8. A 4 × 6 card upon which is written the day's rehearsal schedule and announcements. There should also be several large paper clips to attach the card to the folder and replacements for any clips lost. Sometimes paper clips are also handy for other uses by the director or students during the rehearsal.

9. Memo pad such as in Figure 5-4. It may, at times, be necessary to detain a student for one reason or another, and an excuse can be quickly written for him to give to the next teacher if he will be late for that class. These pads can usually be printed by the school's commercial department or the business office.

10. A calendar, if there is not a wall calendar in the rehearsal room *and*

```
┌─────────────────────────────────────────────────────────────┐
│                    Music Department Memo                     │
│                                                              │
│   TO:                                                        │
│                                                              │
│                                                              │
│   FROM:                                                      │
│                                                              │
│                                                              │
│                                                              │
│                                                              │
│                                                              │
│                                                              │
│   Signed_____        │
└─────────────────────────────────────────────────────────────┘
```

Figure 5-4

in the director's office. This makes quick reference possible when dates must be considered or when questions concerning the next performance, etc. arise.

THE DIRECTOR'S OWN PREPARATION

Herein lies, to a great extent, the secret to the success of the very first rehearsal, as well as each succeeding one. There is no better way for a conductor to get off to a fine beginning than to know his music. A director who repeatedly loses his place in the score or must often stop a rehearsal while he "locates" something will lose the attention and respect of his players. Anyone who, at the first rehearsal, plans to do a selection new to him without a thorough study of it ahead of time, is asking for trouble. To "learn" the score along with the orchestra is a very negative approach to education. The students would be denied the leadership to which they are entitled, and to follow such a practice leads to a breakdown in morale.

The music should be marked regarding dynamics, tempo and tempo changes, phrasing and any trouble spots which the director can predict from his background and/or previous experience. While these items may or may not be touched upon during the first rehearsal, it is well to have it done ahead and then talk about them whenever the time is right. *A good musician is always prepared well ahead of time.*

When the students begin to realize that the director has to take the time to study and know all the parts of a composition, they are usually willing to put in enough practice to become thoroughly acquainted with the one part for which they are responsible. Not only does excellent preparation by the conductor give the students confidence in him, it will also give him the opportunity to pay more attention to the players, especially any new ones with whom he has had only a tryout acquaintance.

ADEQUATE PREPARATION
OF THE MUSIC ITSELF

After choosing the music to be used in the first rehearsal, several things should be done. Some are the responsibility of the director and others can be done by the librarian if it is possible to have that student available before the school year begins. If this is not feasible, the director will have to do them before the first rehearsal. (However, any new music that is not to be used right away can be left until after school begins and the student helper can then take care of the details.)

Director's Responsibilities

If the selection has not been used before, *all* parts should be checked against the full score for errors. Occasionally there may be a few notation errors, repeat marks left out, etc. A small check in the upper right hand corner of the music will indicate that the part has been checked and is correct.

The string parts in the full score should be marked as to bowing and fingering desired. If the director is not a string player, perhaps a teacher of strings in the community can be asked to assist in this matter. Most string teachers are happy to do whatever they can to help players advance and play their parts in the best possible manner. If no one is available for this, the concertmaster should do it. It will be good practice for him, and, working with the conductor, it usually can be done quite well. Sometimes after playing a passage one way, it seems better to do it another way, so this is not something that has only one possible arrangement. However, there are certain things that are basic, especially in bowings, and a student who is advanced enough to be concertmaster should know them. Usually orchestra conductors who are primarily wind players have taken the time to study enough about strings to know the fundamental aspects of playing. If a private string teacher helps out, it can serve as a basis of cooperation in recommending this person as a teacher for those students wishing to take private lessons.

Rehearsal letters or numbers should be checked to be sure that they are accurate in every part. Nothing delays rehearsal more than having to count measures in order that all may begin at the same place. If no such rehearsal aids are in the parts, they *must* be included. No orchestra can rehearse without such help. If numbers or letters are a considerable distance apart, insertion of additional starting points will be very helpful. I use, for example, 4a, 4b or M1, M2, etc. as the case may be. The director can put these extra markings in the score and the librarian or other student helpers can put them in the parts, if desired.

Librarian's Responsibilities

All string parts should be marked as to bowing and fingering, using the marked score as a guide. These should be done in black pencil in case a change is made.

Other important markings should be put in the parts, again from the score. Such things as ritard, tenuto, coda sign, repeat, change of time signature or an especially difficult key change might be circled in red. This will attract attention and be unlikely to be overlooked. However, if the music is borrowed or rented, markings such as the above should not be used. If it is necessary to do any marking, it should be done only with soft black pencil and as lightly as possible to still be visible. All such marks should be erased on every part before the music is returned to the lender.

Music should be checked to be certain that there are enough parts for every player and that all parts are by the same publisher. Experience has shown that different editions of the same work may contain some variations, especially of rehearsal letters or numbers. If a selection has been arranged, it is best not to mix arrangements.

Each piece of music should be identified as belonging to the high school music department. Rubber stamps are most efficient for this purpose. Since most people are right handed, the easiest and quickest manner to do this is to stamp the upper right hand corner and move the parts with the left hand.

All music should be numbered also. The identification stamp may also have a place for a number, which makes it possible to have both items at one place. Numbering will facilitate sorting the music when it is time to replace it in the master folder and return it to the file or shelf. The number system will also reveal very quickly any missing parts. Usually the score is numbered 1 with the strings next. Violin I, Stand I will be 2, Violin I, Stand II will be 3, etc. Some directors prefer the numbering to proceed as in the score: piccolo, flute, oboe, etc. How it is done is of little concern, except that once a system has been decided upon it should be kept the same. Using a red pencil and making the numbers fairly large makes for easy reading.

When I was employed as orchestra director at R. A. Long High School in Longview, Washington, one of the first things I did was to check on the music that was available. There had been an orchestra at the school a few years previously, but immediately preceding my arrival a band and string ensemble were the only instrumental groups. There was some full orchestra music in a cabinet, some of it stamped for identification and some not, and none of it numbered. I decided on the system I wished to use and proceeded to sort it all out and number it. I found some parts to be missing, so replacements were ordered and those numbers skipped were put on the parts when they arrived. Having the parts numbered has always been one of the small details I consider very important, as it saves time and makes for efficient organization of the music.

PREPARATION OF PLAYERS' FOLDERS

After the music has been prepared, it should be placed in the folders that are properly marked as Trumpet I, Clarinet II, etc. These markings should be large and should stand out from the color of the folder itself. A thick felt-tip pen is useful for this purpose, or printed labels can be purchased. In the case of the strings, the additional stand number marking will help the librarian in passing out the folders. String players like to use the same music each time, as most put in a few markings of their own.

Orchestra folders should measure at least 10½ × 13. A 12 × 14 folder is even better, as some orchestral music is rather large. My personal preference is the type of folder with side pockets rather than bottom pockets, as all the loose edges are tucked in. I always have the music placed in the right hand pocket with the left side for other things such as finger charts, memos and instruction sheets, pencils, etc. If there is too much music to be placed in the right pocket, a few selections that are not used too often may be placed in the left, *but right side down*, so that the loose edges are again tucked in. One advantage of having all the music on the right side and information sheets, etc. on the left is that these sheets will not get lost within the music itself.

The sorting rack becomes very useful for whoever places the music in the folders and again takes it out after use. When all the folders have been filled according to directions, they should be placed in the folder cabinet or on a shelf ready to be issued the day of the first rehearsal.

A reminder: Check early to be sure you have enough folders so that you can order more if necessary. There should be one for each part, plus a few spares in case some get left out in the rain! As the supply dwindles, more should be ordered so that there are always some extras.

WHY CORRECT REHEARSAL SEQUENCE
IS SO IMPORTANT

The sequence of the first rehearsal should be planned very carefully by the director. The manner in which he proceeds through the period will, in large part, set the stage for the rest of the year.

There are routine matters that must be taken care of such as seating, introductions, etc., but actual playing should be started as soon as possible. The students will be happier playing than listening to a lecture. It must be remembered that what is played will be sight-reading, and not much detail can be worked out. The idea is to run through part of the music in the folders and let the players see what is in store for them. It is really a preview.

Chapter 6

How to Conduct a First Rehearsal
That Will Excite and Motivate your Players

No matter how experienced the music director, the first rehearsal in the fall is always a challenge. Every conductor is well aware of the fact that the initial impression gained by the players will influence their attitude toward him and toward the organization, and will affect their interest or lack of interest in participating in the group.

IMPORTANT PREPARATIONS

After checking on the physical aspects of the rehearsal room and preparing himself musically well ahead of the opening of school, the director should do the following before the first rehearsal:

1. Chairs, music stands (with folders on them), and the podium should be in place; the room should look "ready" when the students arrive. The director may wish to arrange for a student to do this or to help with it. If this is not done, confusion and time loss will result, as everyone will have to get a chair and stand and put them in place, then the folders will have to be passed out.

   I recall an incident when I was a member of an all-city orchestra. Players from all the city high schools were selected to play in this orchestra which was scheduled to meet each Monday at 4 p.m. at the most centrally located school. I arrived for the very first rehearsal at about 3:40 and most of the players came about that time or soon after. Nothing was set up. There were folding chairs stacked against the wall with some straight chairs scattered here and there. When the director arrived at a little after 4, we were all instructed to grab a folding chair (the straight chairs were assigned to the cello players) and sit anywhere in the section. (We brought our own folding stands.) With the tardiness of the director and the time it took to set up chairs in a somewhat poor arrangement and to pass out the music folders (and each piece to go in them), the rehearsal got underway about 25 minutes late. There were other orchestra directors who assisted with some of the details later in the rehearsal, and some could have arranged to have the chairs set up and even have the music folders (with the music in them) on chairs to assist players in finding their places. This would have hastened the beginning of the actual rehearsal. The conductor came from another school and may have been tied up in traffic, but at least the physical set-up would have been ready and we could have started soon after he arrived.

This was a poor beginning and we all thought that the people in charge were not very well-organized. I've never forgotten this, and I made up my mind then and there that if I ever became an orchestra director I would do all in my power to have things ready at the appointed time and be there to greet the players, especially at the first rehearsal. I realize that this was a bit different from a director's own school orchestra, but with some planning ahead it could have been a much more exciting beginning.

2.   Something should be on the bulletin board; an empty one creates a ''cold'' feeling. Pictures, announcements, articles, lists of books, musical cartoons, etc. are all of interest to the students, and will show them that the director is ''up'' on everything.

3.   If the director's schedule is such that he has any time for office hours, they should be posted on his office door. In the ideal situation, time should be allocated so that he can have conferences with students, parents, or administrators, and also have some planning time.

THE ADVANTAGES OF TEMPORARY SEATING

Seating of the orchestra players at the first rehearsal should be considered temporary. Even though many of the players were in the group the previous year, there could be some seating changes for one reason or another. The director will have to have some time to assess the student's progress following the summer vacation. Also, it is sometimes difficult to place a new player exactly where he belongs just from the tryout or from the junior high school director's recommendation. When one hears him play in conjunction with others around him, a better and fairer perspective is obtained.

The understanding that seating will be temporary for a month or so affords the director the prerogative of changing players around for the best results. It also keeps the players on their toes and makes them put forth their best efforts for keeping their seats or for gaining better ones.

A DIFFERENT METHOD
OF INTRODUCING PLAYERS

I have always made it a point to introduce the players to one another during the first rehearsal. As a rule, there are always some new members. While it may be true that most students know one another, especially if the high school is a rather small one, there is something refreshing for the individual in being noticed. He is temporarily in the spotlight and is conscious of the fact that the director is aware of his contribution to the group.

Certainly, all new members should be introduced to the others. Also, the new players like to know about the rest of the students. The procedure of merely stating the student's name and instrument and letting it go at that does little for the morale of the player or the group. True, this is the quickest way; it takes very little time, but, on the other hand, it also accomplishes little. Over the years I began experimenting, and found that taking the time to do a bit more does wonders for the rapport of the group.

Introducing New Members

Let us assume that there are some new players joining the orchestra. The director, of course, already knows these people from the tryout. Also at his disposal is a certain amount of information gathered from talking with the students and from the tryout blanks. If the director has not worked with the new students from the elementary or junior high, he will have to find out a few facts from their previous director.

Such things as any special honors received, scholarships, attendance at music camp, contest ratings, radio or TV performances, ensemble playing, participation in a junior or civic symphony, etc., are all interesting to the others and can be mentioned in introducing the player. The student will be pleased that the instructor is interested in his accomplishments so far, and the director is silently telling him that he really expects this type of achievement to continue. This establishes both enthusiasm in the student and the desire to prove that the director's trust in him is justified. Some students may not have an outstanding background, but there is always something that can be mentioned. These players should be introduced in alphabetical order to avoid any feeling of being ''last'' and not as important as the others.

Don't Forget Returning Members

To carry this idea further, the same procedure is used in introducing the other members to the newcomers. Since there are many more of these people, the amount of information about them must be reduced and only the high points given.

If the student has been a member of the orchestra for two or more years, the director will know quite a bit about him without having to go through the files. Any special contributions to the orchestra such as holding an office, acting as librarian, stage manager, etc., can be mentioned, as well as those things listed above for the newcomers. Something can be found for each player and this tells him that you, as his director, are proud to have him in the group.

It is a good idea to jot down the players' names in the order of introduction, followed by a note about the comment or comments to be made. (It is up to the director whether he wishes to introduce the continuing members alphabetically or by section in the order in which they are sitting.) It is impractical to depend on one's memory to retain all the facts about the introductions.

The director who has just strings at the first rehearsal can take a few minutes to introduce the woodwind, brass, and percussion players when they come for their first rehearsal. He may not know some of these people, but can find out a bit about them from the band director. All of this really tells each player that he belongs in the ''family'' and is welcomed either as a new addition or as a worthy former member.

A new director obviously will not know the students, and the first year he will probably have to be content with having them introduce themselves or with calling roll.

Referring again to my personal experience in the all-city orchestra (mentioned earlier in this chapter), I remember that the players were not introduced to each other at all. We talked among ourselves before and after rehearsals, and as time went on we got to know each other. Looking back now, I feel that a more friendly atmosphere would have prevailed if a little time had been taken to acknowledge each person. I realize that it would have taken a lot of time to introduce everyone, since it was a large group of about 80; however, it could have been done by sections during the first few rehearsals, with each one just giving his name and high school.

EFFECTIVE USE OF A ROSTER

Every director will keep some form of record of the students in his orchestra. Most schools use grade books and some also use rosters; I have always used both. A grade book is easier to carry about, and the roster can be left in the conductor's folder.

It is most beneficial to have a record, not only of the students' names, but also of addresses, phone numbers, instruments played and class standing (F.,S.,J., Sr.). This information can be on the roster before the first rehearsal. Data for returning students need only be updated from the previous year's record, and the facts concerning the new members can be transferred from the try-out blanks. If the director is also the elementary or junior high director, he will already have the information for the students coming in from these schools; if not, it can be obtained from the office or from the other director.

A moment should be taken to ascertain from each returning student whether or not his address and phone number are the same as last year. Instead of taking this up as a separate item, I have always done it in conjunction with the introductions, since I was addressing the student anyway. Even though this information will be of value later rather than at the first rehearsal, the director again has impressed the student with his interest by wanting to be sure to be able to contact him if necessary. The students should be instructed to inform the director promptly of any changes in address and/or telephone number during the year.

IMPORTANCE OF WARM-UP DRILLS

For the first rehearsal in the fall, the warm-up drills are most essential. It is quite safe to assume that many of the players have not practiced much, if at all, during the summer months. Obviously they are a bit rusty—fingers are stiff, lips are tender. Even their hearing may have somewhat declined—not that they have lost their sense of pitch, but they may have slipped slightly in their habit of paying close attention to it.

The warm-up drills are their first experience at playing in a group again after vacation. Some may have attended a music camp or participated in a summer school orchestra, but these are usually held during the first part of the summer and there quite likely has been a time lapse. The drills will give them the opportunity to get the feel of their instruments again, and of hearing the combined sounds of the orchestra.

The students may be rather shy about playing out because of lack of practice, but they are more likely to use a greater amount of force on the drills than if the rehearsal started with a regular selection. I have always made it a point to have the orchestra play warm-up drills on this occasion at *forte* to help overcome timidness. The players feel more at ease if everyone plays somewhat loudly—they think that perhaps mistakes by individuals may go unnoticed.

The drills help overcome nervousness, limber up fingers and lips, sharpen hearing, and, best of all, get the players in the mood for tackling the first number.

The drills should not be lengthy, as everyone wants to get to the meat of the music as soon as possible; yet they should be intense and have meaning. The warm-up drill does much the same thing that "warming up" does for athletes: conditions them and gets them ready for the main event. This part of the rehearsal should not be neglected.

THE CONTENTS OF THE MUSIC FOLDER

Sometimes directors fail to appreciate the importance of the contents of the music folders for the first rehearsal. Why do merchants spend so much time, effort, and money on window displays? Obviously, it is to show the onlooker what is available inside and so attract him. So it is with the music folder. The student finds in it that which is in store for him in the coming weeks. *What goes into the player's folder for the first look is very important.*

Informational Sheet

The folder should contain a sheet (8½ × 11), typed and duplicated, with all pertinent information the director wants his players to know and to have handy for future reference. This may include tentative performance dates, as well as dates of concerts that the students should plan to attend if at all possible. Also, any rules and regulations the director sets up regarding the orchestra should be listed. (Usually the director has a few of these and later the group members can discuss any others that they might wish to add.) Instructions about having a pencil (with eraser) by the next rehearsal, always looking for the day's schedule on the board, and getting their music in order when they arrive can be included. I have always placed this sheet on the left hand side of the folder and the music itself on the right hand side.

Music

All of the music for the first rehearsal, including warm-up drills, should be in the folders; also, insert some selections that will *not* be used until later rehearsals, plus one or two favorites from the previous year. I have found that putting a medley of show tunes or a couple of light novelty numbers among the standard literature brings smiles to the students' faces as they browse through the various compositions.

All of the semester's music should not be in the folders at this time. Leave some to be passed out later, as it is always interesting to the players to come to a rehearsal and find a new piece of music on the stand.

It is a good idea to have the music for this rehearsal already in the correct sequence. This will allow the students time to read the informational sheet and explore the music itself.

THE PLANNING OF AN EXCITING BEGINNING

How anything is begun often determines how the remainder will go. If a rehearsal gets off to a dull, slow start, lack of preparation and/or lack of enthusiasm may be the chief cause(s). I have found that one of the best ways to generate interest is for the director to show sincere enthusiasm himself. He should not be in his office reading a journal when the students arrive; rather, his presence in the rehearsal room is an effective measure for stimulating eagerness to participate in the rehearsal. This shows the players that he is interested in them and in his work.

When it comes time to actually play, the selection following the warm-up should really excite the players. A method that never fails is to choose a stimulating number, something that can be executed fairly well the first time through. *This is very important.* If a composition is so difficult that the group falls apart at the end of the first phrase, the punch will be gone and from then on it will be an uphill fight for the rest of the session. It is, therefore, necessary that the director give careful thought to what he uses as an opener.

Full Orchestra Selections

I have found any one of the following to be very effective openers.
  1. Andalucia Suite - Lecuona
  2. Beautiful Galathea Overture - Suppe
  3. Cosi fan tutte Overture - Mozart
  4. Danse Bacchanale from *Samson et Dalila* - Saint-Saëns
  5. Farandole from *L'Arlesienne Suite #2* - Bizet
  6. Hoe Down from *Rodeo* - Copland
  7. La Belle Helene Overture - Offenbach
  8. La Reine de Saba - Gounod
  9. L'Italiana in Algeri Overture - Rossini
  10. London Suite - Coates
  11. Orpheus in Hades Overture - Offenbach
  12. Prelude and Fugue - Handel - Kindler
  13. Russian Sailors' Dance from *The Red Poppy* - Gliere
  14. Russlan and Ludmilla Overture - Glinka
  15. Secret Marriage Overture - Cimarosa
  16. Slavonic Dance #8 - Dvorak
  17. Suite for Orchestra (Arr. Ormandy) - Handel
  18. Triumphal March from *Sigurd Jorsalfar* - Grieg
  19. Trumpet Voluntary - Purcell
  20. Zampa Overture - Herold

The above list includes numbers containing varying degrees of difficulty, and is, of course, very incomplete. There are many appropriate selections that can be used. The thing to remember is to start with something with spirit and movement.

String Orchestra Selections

For the director who has just strings at the first rehearsal, one of the following numbers, or something similar, would be suitable for the beginning:
1. Brandenburg Concerto #3 (G Major) - Bach
2. Concerto Grosso Op. 6, No. 7 - Corelli
3. Concerto Grosso Op. 6, No. 2 - Handel
4. Concerto Grosso Op. 3, #8 - Vivaldi
5. Eine Kleine Nachtmusik - Mozart
6. Quartet in F Major - Stamitz
7. Simple Symphony - Britten
8. Sinfonie in D Major - Mendelssohn

I recommend starting out with a string number, as all parts are there and players can hear a complete sound for their first selection. Later in the period string parts of full orchestra numbers can be worked on as time allows.

12 TESTED STEPS
FOR THE FIRST REHEARSAL

Herein lies an important part of the entire semester's work. How the first rehearsal is handled may make a difference in how things go subsequently. No detail, however small, should be considered unimportant.

I have found, over many years of directing high school orchestras, the following 12 steps to be most successful.
1. Be in the rehearsal room when the students begin to arrive. There are many things the director can be doing at this time: getting scores in order on his stand; writing music sequence or information on the board; making a final check on seating arrangements; tightening a loose stand base; or giving a final touch-up of polish to the tuba or a string bass.
2. Welcome students by name as they come in. Those coming in from the lower schools will have to be asked their names if the director has not worked with them before. A new director, of course, will have to ask most of the names; the only ones he'll really know are those he has auditioned. The players should be instructed to sit where they sat last year and to leave vacant the chairs of the graduates. Fill in the gaps when all are present. The new players can be placed where the director feels they may fit in best. It is understood that this seating will be temporary.
3. Give a short welcome message.
4. Introduce all players, giving a brief sketch of each one. Check

addresses and phone numbers as this is done.

5. Ask students to check to be sure they have the right folder on the stand. Occasionally the director (or student who passes out the folders) will be interrupted and make a mistake. To discover this at the "downbeat" is a bit late and can break the mood of the players. Once the "downbeat" comes, they want to play, not wait while parts are exchanged. (This very rarely happens, as the students usually look through their folders when they arrive, but there might be a latecomer.)

6. Tune. At this point, the tuning procedure that will be in effect for all rehearsals should be stated. When the director mounts the podium, if he uses one, and perhaps waves his arm slightly, all tuning ceases. Here he can explain that hereafter all tuning should cease when he steps on the podium. If a director doesn't use a podium, when he steps directly in front of the group or indicates by some gesture that the players recognize, tuning should stop.

7. Conduct warm-up drills. Only a few minutes need be allotted to this. A few comments, even in a joking manner, about their intonation will put players at ease.

8. Read through the opening selection that was chosen carefully. Stop only if absolutely necessary, then be specific about the reason for falling apart. A few minutes of drill on that particular passage at the moment will usually pay off.

9. Read through other numbers on the agenda, remembering that this is all sight-reading.

10. Make any announcements near the end of the period. Included might be such things as plans for the semester (in brief), when to have election of officers, when to have discussion of any rules they wish to talk over, asking for volunteers for librarian(s) if none had been selected in the spring or contacted before school began. Remind the students to read the informational sheet in the folder (if they haven't already done so), and reinforce the parts about having a pencil (with eraser) by next rehearsal and getting their music in order when they come in next time. Take a moment to comment on a thing or two to watch for next time a certain piece is rehearsed, and to tell them how well they did for a first rehearsal.

11. End the rehearsal with a favorite selection from the previous year. This is usually one they liked very much but didn't get to play to the point of being tired of it. This will end the session on a pleasant note; the students will depart with a good feeling, especially if the ones who were in the group the year before feel that they retained much of what they had learned about the piece previously. A new director may not be able to do this if he has not contacted anyone beforehand to find out

a favorite number. However, he can ask at the first rehearsal and perhaps do it for a few subsequent rehearsals.

12. Allow enough time for the students to put their instruments away carefully and to check out folders, if they wish to do so. Also, there must be time to collect the folders not taken home and put them away.

This will be a very full rehearsal, but if every minute is planned carefully, all of these things can be accomplished.

Chapter 7

Key Techniques for Conducting
Productive Orchestra Rehearsals

After successfully getting through the first rehearsal, you are confronted with the problem of handling subsequent rehearsals effectively. It is obvious that each rehearsal must be productive and interesting. Loss of either or both of these objectives will cause the orchestra to lose its potential and eventually its status as a learning and performing unit.

While certain routines or procedures are necessary in each rehearsal, care must be taken to see that this sameness is not a cause of lack of motivation and stagnation.

KEEPING YOUR GROUP AT ITS PEAK

Keeping the group at its peak during the entire rehearsal time will insure maximum return in the form of achievement and interest. If you can instill in the players the idea that each rehearsal should be treated as if it were the *last* rehearsal before a concert (in which every effort is made to miss nothing and to perfect everything) there should be little trouble in motivation and achievement.

Certain aspects of the rehearsal need special attention in order to remain fresh and useful. Saying the same remark in the same way can soon result in a sort of hypnosis and so fail to hit its mark—the students' ears. A bit of forethought as to how to say something is important; many times students will remember *what* is said because of *how* it is said. Comparison with the area of sports in relationship to timing, cooperation, striving toward perfection, etc., will have a positive effect on the group and will help to promote a healthy rapport between you and the players. The alteration of gestures and facial expressions will relieve monotony because the players must watch carefully and not play by habit.

In order to combat a routine that becomes boring, you should be constantly alert to the use of new approaches and ways of executing rehearsals. While certain basic aspects must be maintained in order to achieve the desired objectives, different approaches will have a psychological effect on the players and release enthusiasm, interest, and alertness. A bit of humor injected whenever possible has a very positive effect on the morale of the group and helps relieve tensions.

A stimulating beginning sets the tone for a rehearsal. Following are 13 other specific suggestions that will help in making each rehearsal a successful one:

THE IMPORTANCE OF
THE DIRECTOR'S PREPARATION

The results of each rehearsal will be determined to a great extent by how well you are prepared. By preparation I mean knowing the score note for note; this is a must for every composition. In addition, you should have clipped to the upper left corner of your folder a 4×6 card that contains the precise routine for that particular rehearsal as well as any announcements to be made. (I have found that using two paper clips attached to the left side of the folder allows the card to project above the top of the folder. This will prevent shuffling around in the music to find the card.) Besides saving time, it will be evident to the players that you are organized and not wasting time, nor should they. A typical example of the content of the card is Figure 7-1.

There are many advantages in having the schedule on the chalkboard as well as on a card, as explained in Chapter 3. Generally the board is behind the director, and having the card makes it easier to see what comes next without having to turn around.

Many instrumental and vocal directors of my acquaintance now make use of this system of putting the day's schedule on the board and having a card on the conductor's stand or folder for easy reference. All of them agree that it has improved their rehearsals by saving precious time for actual work.

If you are well-prepared, not only will the rehearsal move ahead rapidly, but the confidence in you established with the players will give them added incentive to do their best. No director is ever overprepared. The old adage "The music should be in the conductor's head and not his head in the music," is very true.

1. Warm-up drill—key of D Major, Concert   9:00
      Scale—2 octaves at Moderato, Allegro
      & Presto; legato & staccato

2. Zampa Overture—beginning to G   9:05
      Watch dynamics

3. Dance of Comedians—sight-read   9:15

4. Beethoven, Symphony = 1—1st Movement   9:25
      Spot check C-G, Winds
                    C-G, Strings
                    Tuti
                    K-M, Horns & Woodwinds
                    T to end, Tutti

5. Announcements: Concert Tues. changed from 7:30 to 8 p.m.
      Strings meet in Room 106,
      Winds & Percussion, Room 109.
      Stage manager see me a minute after class.

6. Hopak—up to tempo, polish   9:45

7. Dimiss   9:50

Figure 7-1

THE PSYCHOLOGICAL EFFECT OF PUNCTUALITY

Punctuality is the key word for any rehearsal. Much time is wasted by starting late. This means that you, as well as the players, must be ready to "go" on time. Always start on the dot, even if only half your group is there at first. It should not take very long for the members of the group to catch on to what you mean by punctuality. It may mean that students must hurry a bit from their previous class in order to get to the rehearsal room, get their instruments out, put music in order from the schedule on the board, and warm up a bit. This is not all bad. Students need training in moving along and being prompt. If rehearsals begin late, players will not make an effort to be there on time and will come in later and later. If the room is "set up" and you are there ready to start, the students will be motivated to be ready at the proper time also.

How a Rehearsal Should Begin

At the precise time you have established, the concertmaster stands. This means all individual playing stops at once. The oboe, or piano if strings only are present, gives the concert A and tuning takes place, carefully and rapidly. (A tuning fork or electric tuner may be used if one is available.) After allowing about two minutes for the tuning, ascend the podium or give a signal for tuning to cease. No rapping of the baton is necessary; all players can watch the front since their eyes need not really be on their instruments to tune. Immediately begin the rehearsal.

What You Can Do About Tardiness

At times students will be late for various, usually acceptable, reasons. I have always made it understood that they owe me an explanation. Should lateness occur too many times with flimsy excuses, however, something positive should be done. One way to attack the problem is to acknowledge the person's arrival by saying, "Good morning, John," without stopping the rehearsal. Nothing more is usually necessary; this will tell him and the orchestra members that were aware of his absence from the beginning. While this is done in a polite manner, the implications are there. Usually this is more attention than the student cares to have, and the incident is not likely to recur. However, if it persists, it should be handled as an individual disciplinary matter.

IMPORTANT RESPONSIBILITIES
OF EACH PLAYER

Each player must realize that the success of any rehearsal depends upon his contributions to the group. The responsibilities are numerous. One is no more important than another; therefore, the following list of 13 responsibilities is not in order of preference.

The student must:

1. Be punctual.
2. Have his instrument in good working condition. In the string section this means proper strings in good condition, bow with adequate hair, rosin and extra strings readily available, and pegs adjusted properly for easy tuning. Woodwind players should have reeds in good shape and pads properly adjusted. All brass valves should be working smoothly. The large instruments and percussion equipment usually belong to the school, and the responsibility of the student ends by informing you of any necessary repairs. However, the people using these instruments must be made aware of the procedure for taking care of them and of their responsibility for doing so.
3. Have a black, soft pencil and eraser. Students should carry one in the instrument case and one in the folder so there will always be one on hand. They should be instructed to mark any change in the music at the time it is discussed and *never* rely on memory.

4. Have mutes readily available. There are different types of string mutes, but whichever type is used should be either on the instrument or on the person (if on the stand, it can easily be knocked off). Brass players' mutes should be next to them on the floor. Shuffling through cases just before mutes are needed not only wastes time but disrupts the rehearsal.
5. Practice music on his own as much as necessary in order to perform it to the best of his ability.
6. Treat sheet music with care and mend any torn parts. Any loss should be reported immediately to the librarian for payment and replacement.
7. See that his music folder and all selections are at every rehearsal. This is not only necessary in the case of players who have individual parts but also for those who share folders. No players should be required to read three on a stand.
8. Close music folders at the end of rehearsal (with all selections inside the pockets). This enables the librarian to pick up folders quickly and in the preferred order.
9. Check out any folders to be taken home. A checklist can be posted on the side of the folder cabinet with names and dates. The student can check it whenever he takes music home. You then have a record of who has what. Sometimes students wish to check out folders but leave them in the cabinet until after school. They should be reminded to *always* check them out; otherwise you will assume they are misplaced. The checklist form can be duplicated and a student can have the assignment of changing it every week or month, as you wish. The librarian sometimes has this duty.
10. Listen quietly when explanations about the music are given. Very often suggestions given one section might pertain to other sections somewhere else in the composition, and students can learn many pertinent facts about techniques and music itself by listening. You should draw attention to this.
11. Not play on his instrument while explanations or instructions are being given. Many string players have a bad habit of plucking certain passages or open strings to see if they are in tune. Any such disturbance delays adequate presentation, since you will most likely have to ask the person or persons to stop and then begin what you were saying again.
12. Leave quickly and quietly after rehearsal. This is especially important if there is another performing group following; it will enable them to start on time.
13. Inform you of any extended illness or other situation that will make it impossible for him to attend rehearsals for a period of time or to

participate in a concert. Unless some dire emergency arises, advance notice should always be given so that you will know what the situation is and others can be assigned to take over any important solos, should this be necessary.

AN EFFECTIVE TUNING PROCEDURE

While any orchestra needs to be in tune with itself, this is especially true of the high school orchestra. The players are far from professionals and one of their chief obstacles is intonation; hence a well-tuned orchestra will do better at playing in tune.

Strings

Tuning should be done efficiently, yet with a minimum of time. Upon hearing the concert A from the oboe (or clarinet, in the absence of oboe), the strings should be tuned first with the other sections remaining silent. Young high school players need to listen carefully when tuning their instruments. If the winds are allowed to tune simultaneously, accuracy of the strings will be more difficult to obtain because of the volume of sound. It can also be helpful if each string section tunes separately. This is most effective with a large string section or at the beginning of the school year.

Woodwinds

Next the woodwinds should tune. Quite often the flutes and clarinets have the most difficulty in getting together on the A. A student playing the oboe may be slightly out of tune in giving the A, even though this instrument is one of the most reliable. The woodwinds may still have problems even if they all have the right A; certain ranges may be slightly off pitch and players have to learn to remedy this by changing the embouchure.

Brass

The brass should tune last. Also, they should be instructed to tune at a *piano* level. Nothing will be accomplished by "blowing their heads off," as the louder they tune, the less they can hear.

Following this the entire group should sound concert A together, but *softly*. All of this should not take more than a couple of minutes.

Subsequent Tuning

You will, of course, indicate any retuning during the rehearsal if conditions make it necessary. Gradually players will become experienced and will be able to tune quietly during the actual playing and will be accurate. However, this procedure cannot be hurried. It should be stressed that at no time should mass tuning be done unless so requested. For everyone to tune at random can create nothing but confusion.

Once proper methods have been established the players will get into this routine, and by the end of the first semester will be able to speed up the tuning process without a drop in accuracy. By late in the year, some orchestras may be able to tune all sections at once; however, this should not be done unless accuracy can be maintained.

VALUES IN OCCASIONAL CHANGES
IN SEATING ARRANGEMENTS

As a student in orchestra, I switched from violin to viola and later also played cello. Remembering that I had experienced an entirely new feeling of sound in the different locations, I decided to try some switching of sections now and then when I became an orchestra director myself.

Most inexperienced players pay attention only to their own parts. Occasionally exchanging places with another section gives them the opportunity of hearing other parts more clearly and makes them more conscious of what other players are doing.

Very few high school orchestras are arranged with the first and second violins facing each other. The reason is obvious: high school players do not have the power and bow control to draw out the sound as professionals do, nor do they, in most cases, have outstanding instruments. Having them playing *into* the orchestra is asking for an imbalance in the strings. However, putting them there for a short time and putting the violas or cellos next to the firsts can be good for all concerned. One can also reverse the violas and cellos from outside to inside, as well as change the two violin sections. Usually if I move the cellos I also move the basses so they are still behind them. Once in a while they can be separated and so have to depend solely on themselves.

This shifting around applies mainly to the string sections; however, at times I have also rotated the woodwind and brass players, as well as moved the percussion to the center or to the other side.

Aside from being refreshing and helping to keep rehearsals interesting, I have found that a result of this "musical chairs" is more in-depth listening by the players. This is one of our objectives. A better blend of the whole orchestra can be achieved by occasional use of this technique.

I always tell the players why these switches are made, so they know I want them to experience the sounds in the different locations. Also, they should be told about the plans a day ahead rather than taking rehearsal time to reshuffle them. It will take a little extra time to get settled anyway. If the librarian knows ahead of time, the music will be on the right stands and a minimum of time will be lost in getting started.

Under no circumstances should these "switches" be used at performances. Stick to the established seating pattern then.

HOW MUCH TIME
SHOULD BE DEVOTED TO WARM-UPS?

Even though the warm-up is only a small part of the rehearsal period, it is very important. It establishes attention and builds a positive frame of mind. Ears are alerted to sound and thoughts are transferred from the previous subject to orchestra. No more than five minutes need be allocated for this purpose. If properly done, this short period can be interesting and beneficial to the entire rehearsal.

Warm-up procedures must be altered frequently in order to keep the routine, which it is, refreshing. Each period should include some scale work with the transposing instruments playing concert pitch; this will train these players in the art of transposition. Chords, intervals, staccato, legato, rhythms, articulation, and bowing exercises are things that can be done. Using different dynamics provides a change and also gives practice in achieving good results in this area. (Examples of drills are given in Appendix I.) Variety regarding the procedure is the key to success.

WAYS OF DEVELOPING GOOD INTONATION

Perhaps nothing is more frustrating than the problem of intonation. Since it is possible for players to play *every* note out of tune, you should be constantly alert and demand, without let-up, that attention be given to proper intonation at all times. The old phrase, "Play in tune," gets worn out very rapidly and soon ceases to be heard. You can approach the problem verbally in several different ways. Useful are remarks such as these: "Let's improve on the intonation," "Can we stay within the key?" "Let's raise the third of the chord," "Play it at the 'top' of the range and make it more brilliant," "Listen carefully. Try to hear the note before playing it."

Four Tested Ways to Improve Intonation

1. One of the best ways to get started right on a new selection is to play it slowly. This does not mean so slow that the musical sense is distorted. I know it is difficult for director and students alike to hold back, but young players simply cannot find notes rapidly *and* play them in tune at first.

2. If the warm-up includes drills in the keys of the selections to be rehearsed, the intonation is likely to improve. The players, through these warm-ups, get the key established in their minds and the matter of tonality becomes the focal point. This is essential for good intonation.
3. There are times when it is useful to sing a passage (if within the voice range) before playing it. There is nothing wrong in having instrumentalists sing on a few spots (a neutral syllable is best). If they can sing it, they can usually play it in tune. If this has been included in their early training, there is less embarrassment.
4. Sometimes each section should work out an intonation problem separately, just for a few moments. At the time, no vibrato should be used. Vibrato, especially in young string players, is actually playing a bit "out of tune," and use of this when trying to overcome intonation problems may only compound them; once the intonation has improved, the use of vibrato may be resumed.

It is best to avoid having an individual play a passage alone. Playing together gives confidence; each player will be less nervous and more likely to play in tune. Also, less time is lost. Any persistent cases can be dealt with in private and thus avoid embarrassment to the player.

Even if the flutes are a bit out of tune, it is best to have them play together; or first flute and oboe if they play the same part. They need to be in tune with each other anyway, and should try to hear the correct pitch and blend it.

The most essential element is to develop the players' ears and teach them how to listen. They must be made aware that good intonation depends upon building each tone in sequence. If a tone is correct, the next one is more likely to be in tune, since each is built upon the previous one. Sometimes a few moments taken to practice some troublesome intervals will pay off. Always make this an aspect of all rehearsals.

USEFUL SUGGESTIONS ON
HOW TO IMPROVE TONE QUALITY

One of the many problems that the average high school orchestra encounters is one of tone quality. In listening to many high school orchestras, I have found that frequently little or no attention was being given to the quality of the tone of the group. There was, in many cases, thin string tone, weak woodwind sound, and blatty quality from the brass section. The three never quite blended.

While final tone quality must be suited to each specific selection, practice in development of a good tone can be done as a part of the warm-up period. There is no reason why intonation and tone quality cannot be dealt with while playing a scale or a selected drill. The more you can accomplish at the same time, the further ahead the group will be. The outcome must be a beauty of sound, blended and balanced among the sections of the ensemble. Following are specific ways of making this possible.

Professional Tone Quality Expectations Unrealistic

It is impractical to expect students of high school age to produce a quality of tone comparable to that of a symphony orchestra. In the first place, the instruments themselves cannot compare with those of professionals. Also, the mature symphony players have years of training and experience behind them. Therefore, I do not advise listening to tapes or recordings of professional symphonies *with emphasis upon matching tone quality exactly*. (More is said about this later in the chapter.) Each group will have its own level of achievement in this respect; the objective is to produce the best tone possible.

In dealing with tone quality, you will need to give special attention to each section on specific problems.

Strings

Resonance can be lost when the strings are played softly. This is because, psychologically, when a player reduces the pressure upon the bow, he unconsciously does the same to the finger pressure producing the note. At once the tone fizzles and the notes are no longer clear and distinct. Also, in soft passages, the bow is correctly moved away from the bridge and toward the fingerboard; this also cuts down on the resonance as there is not as much of the string that can vibrate. The combination of these two factors is the cause of much of the soft tone problem.

The bow technique being the correct procedure, one must deal with the finger pressure in this situation. As the pressure on the bow decreases, the pressure on the finger playing the note must be increased. Tell the string players that under normal volume of, say *forte*, there exists an equal division of pressure between left hand and the bow, 50%-50%. If the bow pressure is reduced to 25%, the left hand pressure increases to 75%. In other words, there must be present a combined total of 100% between left hand and right hand.

The strings should, during warm-up periods, make use of such simple devices as those in Figures 7-2 through 7-5.

In addition to the four brief examples given, any orchestral passage can be used—play it softly and work for good tone quality.

Proper Use of Vibrato

Vibrato also has much to do with tone quality. This means not pressure, but the speed with which it is executed. The students should be directed to observe

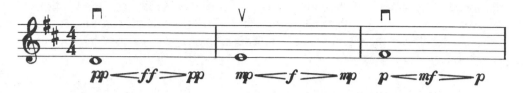

Figure 7-2

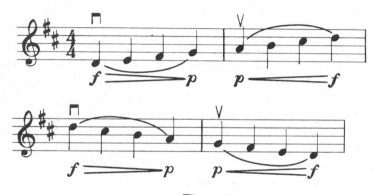

Figure 7-3

Figure 7-4

Figure 7-5

the speed of the vibrato of the violin, viola, cello, and bass players. Observation will reveal that the larger the instrument (therefore, the thicker and longer the strings), the slower the vibrato becomes. This slowness is necessary in order to give the tone time to vibrate.

This rule must be applied by each player to each of his strings. For example, a vibrato on the E string on a violin must be faster than that on the G string. Unfortunately, many high school string players, unless they are studying with a good private teacher, tend to vibrato at the same rate of speed on each string. This results in rather poor tone quality. A good procedure for helping to remedy this situation is to have each section play alone. Direct them to play the same finger on each string, using the same vibrato speed. Then have them do it again, increasing or decreasing speed, depending upon which direction they are play- ing. This should be done from time to time, and eventually, as they recognize the difference, it will become automatic to vary the speed on the different strings.

While professionals can be vibrating before the bow is set in motion, high school students should play each succeeding note without use of vibrato for a split second (actually only long enough to ascertain that the pitch is correct) before applying vibrato for the remainder of the value of the note. There is little advantage in gaining a good tone, if the intonation is lost. As they develop skill, they can use their vibrato more professionally.

An error that I have observed is that many string players try to vibrato when playing eighth or faster notes. This is nearly impossible unless the tempo is quite slow, because there is not ennough time to move the hand back and forth to produce a vibrato.

Vibrato is not used at all times, even on long tones. In many selections, for certain effects, vibrato can be discontinued for a passage, or for part of one. This can give a variety to the tone quality and add to the interest in listening to the work.

Correct Use of the Bow

When a loud or bright tone quality is desired, the bow should move closer to the bridge and the pressure upon the bow must be increased as it moves from the frog to the tip. The faster the bow moves, the more pressure should be applied. The slower it moves, the more the pressure must be released near the frog, or a scratching sound will result.

A few minutes on bow control with the strings alone with long, slow bows on whole notes (playing a scale at the same time) will do much to develop a good sustained tone. Considerable time should be devoted to this practice if the string section meets separately during part of the week, or in sectional rehearsals.

One of the best drills for tone control and quality is that given in Figure 7-2. This will be especially difficult to do on the up-bow, since the *decrescendo* will come in the lower part of the bow. Many times this occurs in orchestral music because it is not always possible to bow a sequence or phrase with the bow near the tip on a soft passage. The bow should be allowed to glide toward the fingerboard to help diminish the sound; also, the wooden part of the bow should be tipped a little toward the fingerboard on soft passages.

In playing slurred notes, pressure of the bow must be increased from the middle to the tip in order to maintain the same level of volume (unless a *decrescendo* is indicated). The reverse is true on the up-bow or the last series of notes tend to be louder and of a different quality.

Appendix I contains successful tone-quality development drills that should be a part of the warm-up period from time to time.

Pizzicato: How to Obtain Best Results

In playing pizzicato, young players usually produce a sound that can only be described as a "thud." True pizzicato, unless specified to be played *secco* (dry), should ring and bounce. The best way to achieve this is to lift the hand and arm in a graceful upturn, press the left finger or fingers down hard, and vibrate the note or notes as the strings are plucked. In this instance the student cannot follow the previous suggestion regarding vibrato when bowing, as there is not enough time. Slow practice for intonation should be undertaken before the passage is taken up to tempo. Players should also be instructed to pluck the strings one to two inches from the end of the fingerboard nearest the bridge (further for the larger instruments). Some players like to have the right thumb against the fingerboard when playing pizzicato, but a better tone is produced with more freedom of hand and arm. The combination of vibrating for the duration of the note and plucking away from the end of the fingerboard will bring forth a pizzicato tone that is as light, bouncy, and springy as a ping-pong ball.

In rapid passages, of course, vibrato cannot be used. When a *secco* pizzicato is required, the strings may be plucked near the end of the fingerboard and at times without vibrato. Never should plucking be done between the bridge and fingerboard where the bow travels, and never with the fingernails. (String players should always have fingernails on both hands clipped quite short.)

It is up to you as orchestra director, whether or not you are a string player, to watch for all the foregoing points in development of string tone.

Brass

In the brass section there is usually no fear of their playing too softly. Instead the question arises—how loud is loud, and when does the tone cease to be a tone of quality? If the brass players are also in the band, special attention needs to be given to this since there is quite a difference between playing in a band and in an orchestra. It is well to remember that since fewer players are required for orchestra than for band, reliance on others playing the same part is no longer possible. (This, of course, is also true of the woodwinds.) This thought alone can create a poor tone quality resulting from fear. This is true particularly in the soft or exposed passages. In the loud portions, the tendency is to overblow and the result may be a blatty tone.

Good Brass Tone—How to Achieve It

The brasses should practice long, soft tones. Many of the brass parts in orchestral playing consist of sustained notes, especially in the French horns. Care needs to be taken that all brass players learn to "hold back" except where the melodic line is concerned. A good approach is: when not involved in the melody, brass is a supporting section and must abstain from the spotlight and allow another section or instrument to shine. Each brass player should become aware that he is part of a balanced group. Projecting beyond the level of the others and standing out as a separate unit means his tone quality (not only dynamics) is out of balance.

When brasses (and also woodwinds) have solo passages, beating should be somewhat adjusted so that they have ample time for breathing; otherwise, the tone will suffer.

Brass players should be instructed, when playing sustained *ff* or *f* passages, to play them *ff-f* or *f-mf*, since the moving parts are elsewhere and must not be covered. This will create a tone of good quality and an overall blend of beauty.

Woodwinds

The woodwinds, in contrast to the brass, usually play too softly and timidly. Since the number of players is usually reduced even more than in the brass section, there is more tendency to become frightened, producing a shaky, weak tone.

Problems Concerning the Bassoon

The higher range of the bassoon should be avoided unless the player is outstanding. A good tone quality in this range is difficult at best, and usually not within the ability of the average high school bassoonist. Better to drop the part an octave, if possible, or substitute with viola or cello.

Overcoming Difficulties

I have found that asking the woodwinds to play out, that is, increasing the dynamic mark by about one-half, will give them a bit more confidence. The tone will become more even and have a richer quality. This also makes it possible for them to be heard. During the warm-up period, long tones played at *f* or above will do much to develop a richer, fuller, and more even tone quality.

The many specific techniques for each woodwind instrument regarding development of tone are too numerous to be discussed here. In many cases students will have had some private instruction by the time they enroll in the high school orchestra; however, it is your responsibility to be able to help those who are not getting instruction outside of school. The establishment of confidence in each player will do much to improve tone quality.

Examples of Substitutions and/or Additions

There are instances when, because of inadequate or insufficient players on one or two instruments, a solution must be found to the problem of bringing out a melody or important inner part. It is possible, within limitations, to improve the tone quality by adding to the existing instruments or section, or by substituting. Care must be taken to be sure that what is added will blend, or the result may be opposite from what is desired. No matter how it is done, some change in timbre will result. The question you must ask yourself is whether or not substitution or addition will improve the general presentation of the composition without affecting the composer's idea of sound. An example might be a cello section of four players, two of whom play quite well and the other two rather weakly. If there are sufficient violas and their part can be covered by a few, there is no reason why some of the viola players can't play with the cellos on certain passages, provided these are within the viola range. The reverse can also be done, if necessary. Simple transposition will make this possible.

Another possibility is to substitute muted trumpet for oboe, or add it to a weak oboe. (It is best not to use cornets in orchestra, if possible; trumpets give a much more positive and solid tone.) Several instruments can be substituted for bassoon, but the quality will be different, of course. Viola or cello were mentioned before; also, trombone, bass clarinet, or baritone can be used. Flutes can help the first violins in the higher register, etc.

Any of these or other changes should be considered only when, for some reason or another, the quality of the tone or volume needs to be improved. An uneasy player or section will produce a better tone if some help is provided. Experience will help solve problems of this nature with the means at hand.

**POSITIVE SOLUTIONS TO
COMMON RHYTHMIC PROBLEMS**

As a rule, with the average high school orchestra rhythm presents a greater challenge during rehearsals than any other aspect of the music. Generally players are able to master the notes quicker than the rhythm. I have found, over the years, that a particularly troublesome spot can be improved with a few minutes of careful analysis and drill, which may have to be repeated from time to time. If what they are doing wrong is explained to the students, it is easier for them to correct it than if they are just told to count. The first step, of course, is to determine the trouble; the second is how best to approach the problem. Third, a correction must be executed, and fourth, it must fit into the general composition as it is intended.

Below are three common rhythmic problems and solutions that are effective:

1. While simple at a glance, Figure 7-6 is often played incorrectly.

Figure 7-6

The players tend to cut the fourth beat short—in a sense rushing the last beat in anticipation of the next measure. If the passage is legato, simply ask the players to "stretch" the last beat. Have them mark their music with a dash or "ten" (Figure 7-7).

Figure 7-7

If the passage is to be played staccato, have them perform it in the manner shown in Figure 7-8 with a "dead" spot between each note.

Figure 7-8

With the strings this requires a complete stop of the bow, or, in some cases, a lift off the string. In the winds this does not necessitate particular attention because the moment a player ceases to blow, the tone stops. Even in such short notes there should be a definite resonance, not merely a sound.

2. Another figure usually needing attention is the dotted eighth followed by the sixteenth as in Figure 7-9.

Figure 7-9

Often young players will begin to get sloppy after one or two continuous measures, and soon it sounds as straight eighth notes or two triplets ♩ ♪. An extremely helpful solution is presented in Figure 7-10. Place it on the chalkboard.

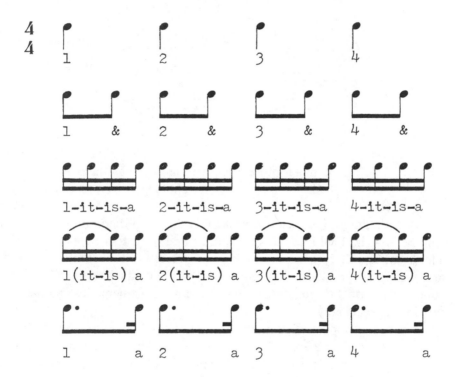

Figure 7-10

Upon close examination, Figure 7-10 is nothing more than a simple exercise in fractions. The entire orchestra should recite these rhythms together, because sooner or later each section will encounter this. All rhythmic problems can be solved much more quickly if the students recite (or sing on a neutral syllable) the particular trouble spot.

3. Another common rhythmical error is that of the playing of triplets. Usually they are hurried and the last note of the three is not given its full 1/3 value, causing an irregular rhythm. Sometimes students will tend to pause slightly after each group. Have them again recite or sing on a neutral syllable (Figure 7-11 and Figure 7-12).

1- o-let 2- o-let 3- o-let

Figure 7-11

1-(o)-let 2-(o)-let 3-(o)-let

Figure 7-12

This is much more effective than saying ''ta ta ta.'' The word ''let'' on the last note will be the right length, as it takes longer to say than ''ta.''

Any rhythmic figure can be broken down, simplified, so that the student can see how it should go. Time should be allocated in rehearsals for such minidrills, especially when learning a new selection. Be certain that the drills have solved the problem, then drill on the part played correctly. Never should sloppy or incorrect rhythm be ignored. Rhythm is mathematics and there is no margin for inaccuracy.

One last comment: Players should never be permitted to tap their feet. Let them move the big toe ever so slightly within the shoe if they need to, but the baton should do the ''beating.'' Toe-tapping is a bad habit, showing immaturity, and once established is very difficult to break.

WHEN SHOULD YOU
TAPE-RECORD YOUR GROUP?

Every orchestra will find some opportunity to make use of a tape recorder. When is the correct time to use this device? Never when beginning work on a new selection; it can be too discouraging. There are at least four times when the recorder can be used to good advantage in reinforcing the work being done.

Pinpointing Inaccuracies

When repeated suggestions and drills concerning intonation, rhythm, or tone quality do not produce desired results, the tape recorder can act as another voice speaking. Let the students hear for themselves a passage that is out of tune or played with incorrect rhythm. How can they possibly dispute what they hear? There are times when a group may question comments made, but never a tape. If the tape recorder is an excellent one, the same can be done in regard to tone quality. If the reproduction capability of the recorder is inferior in this respect, it is best not to stress this too much but to rely on the ears when playing.

Helping Articulation

Students are often unable to realize that they are not playing cleanly. This is because there is much sound around them in addition to their own playing; in a sense they are too close. To tape a sloppy passage will reveal the articulation problem in a way no verbal comment can equal. Several tapings of the same spot can measure the progress for the players until the desired results have been attained.

Deciding on Performance Readiness

Tape an entire selection after it has been polished. Play it back and the orchestra becomes the audience; they now hear themselves as others will hear them. They should be reminded that the presentation will not be exactly the same as when they perform in a gym, auditorium, or wherever, but it will give them an idea of how they come across. Will they be satisfied to present themselves in two weeks or whenever they are to perform? Where are the weak spots? As a learning experience let them be critical and locate the parts that should be improved. Believe me, the next rehearsal will show a noticeable upswing in attention and accomplishment. Sometimes tape recordings can be made during dress rehearsal at the actual site of the performance, and these can be of help; not much actual changing can be done at the last minute, but some adjusting is possible.

Complimenting

I use the tape recorder at times to demonstrate something the orchestra has done exceptionally well, i.e., interpretation, mastery of a technically difficult passage, blending of groups of instruments or sections, etc. The time spent in this manner is well worth it. Rapport is at its best, and the will to do even better becomes very evident.

Care should be taken that the tape recorder is not overused. Too much taping and playing back will absorb valuable rehearsal time. Moderation is a good watchword.

USE OF PROFESSIONAL
TAPES AND RECORDINGS

Unfortunately, sometimes professional tapes and/or recordings are used with negative results. Students often feel that they must match the tone quality, balance, and virtuosity of what is heard, and feel that they just can't do it. True, they should work toward this end, but only to the extent that their abilities allow, and should not be pushed beyond what they can do. This is not to say that they should not be listening to professional presentations; they should, at every opportunity. This is very helpful in their overall musical growth.

Now and then a recording can be played when a group starts out on a new selection, just to get the idea of how it sounds. This can be particularly helpful with contemporary music or something with unusual rhythms, etc. There are at least nine other good reasons for using professional recordings in rehearsals to demonstrate:

1. Precision of attacks and cut-offs
2. Phrasing
3. Dynamics
4. Intonation
5. Rhythmic patterns
6. Articulation
7. Style
8. Accompanying the melodic line
9. Accompanying a soloist

How to Preview

Always listen to any taped or recorded performance in advance to be sure it will serve the correct purpose. I recall an incident that occurred when I was playing in the all-city high school orchestra. The group was having difficulty with a unison string passage in *March Slave* by Tschaikowsky. The director quickly looked around and found a recording of it by a major symphony and put it on the record player. What an embarrassment to him and the orchestra when an incorrect rhythmical presentation was revealed!

Again, caution must be exercised in the use of this type of material. Used occasionally and for definite purposes, it can be of considerable educational value in rehearsals, as well as adding interest and variety.

PRAISE VS. CRITICISM

There is no orchestra that, in the mind of the conductor, plays perfectly. Thus, criticism is a natural aspect of rehearsing. It is through this that the orchestra improves. He who does not correct (that is, criticize), soon loses his stature as a leader. The trick lies in how much criticism to give and how it should be done.

Constructive Criticism a Must

Constructive criticism is the most successful. Players do have to be corrected, but it can be done without sarcasm or constant negative remarks. To jump hard on a player or section in front of the entire group will, at times, result in the reverse effect from that which is desired. Players can "freeze" and not play well at all if they are embarrassed by being singled out.

Players should always be informed of the error and suggestions given for the remedy. The remark, "Play it again, but this time correctly," is of little value. Far better to say, "Let's take it from letter L and watch the D# carefully." You are really criticizing the playing of a certain passage, but at the same time taking positive action to improve it. Another approach is to compliment the good portion of a shaky passage while dealing with the weak part as well. Sometimes a critical look toward a section will let them know that something wasn't just right. Stop playing only for major things; continual stopping breaks up the music too much and players lose the flow.

Praise Instead of Criticize

There are times when it is good to stop the orchestra in order to praise the students' playing instead of criticize. This "shot in the arm" will make that particular rehearsal stand out in the minds of the young performers; they will know that you realize that they have been trying to improve and to remember the things you have told them.

I've always made it a policy to find something to praise at *every* rehearsal. The students will usually see to it that this is possible; for the most part they really want to do well. Both praise and criticism help in achieving the final objective—playing the music to the best of the group's ability and as closely as possible to the composer's desires.

PROCEDURES FOR CLOSING
EACH REHEARSAL

Ending a rehearsal is somewhat akin to the landing of a jet plane. Preparations must be made ahead of time. A successful landing means another take-off is possible. Likewise, a good conclusion of a rehearsal sets the mood for the next one.

There is nothing more irritating to the players than to be playing away when suddenly, in the middle of a phrase, the bell indicating the end of the period shatters the beauty of the musical sound. Rarely will it happen that the pitch of the bell fits the chord the orchestra is playing! Musicians do not like to "drop" a phrase in the middle. Also, this causes an undue rush in getting instruments put away. Speed here could be responsible for damage to an instrument. Care should be taken in putting instruments away, and care does take time.

Five Key Points for Successful Conclusion

1. Plan to ease into the closing portion by playing something in the finishing stages of polish. Not only will the students enjoy giving it an "extra" bit of luster, but the "stop and go" routine experienced earlier in the rehearsal while working on less-prepared selections will be eliminated. In the final analysis, music is heard in its entirety, and the players should also perform it in that manner when possible. As an added incentive, here is a time to make use of the tape recorder. Tape the selection at the close of the period and hold the "playback" until the next day. They will be motivated by looking forward to hearing it.

2. Allow sufficient time for making announcements. A good habit to establish is to run through the announcements, timing them. In this way you will know exactly how much time to plan on. I've found that the best time for them is just before the closing selection. The logic behind this is that the players are anxious to get into the final number and will listen carefully to what is said. Also, by waiting until near the end of the rehearsal, the retention may be better since an entire period of rehearsing will not have elapsed after announcements were made.

3. Sometimes give a preview of the next day's rehearsal. As part of the announcements, entice the players with the title of a new selection to be passed out the next day when this is going to be done. At times tell them that the next day they will get to play a favorite number that has been put aside for a while, or they will get to choose the final selection. Don't always tell them—sometimes surprise them! If this sort of thing is done now and then, it will stimulate interest.

4. Allow time to assess accomplishments and failures during the rehearsal just concluded. Do not plan to take more than a minute for this. Bring up the negative items: in such and such selection, between letters D and F we need to improve intonation; difficult parts are for

2nd Clarinet, 2nd Violins, and French Horns, etc. Now zoom in with the positive accomplishments and agitate your voice a bit—speak with some excitement because you really mean it. The sense of pride that the players feel cannot be measured other than by their smiles and actions as they leave the room. Every director should observe the facial expressions and listen to the remarks made by the students as they leave. These can be most informative.

5. Finish before the bell rings. A good habit is to time each selection for future programming. This information can also be very helpful in closing the rehearsal. You will not be likely to run out of time. Rapport between the music department and other school departments suffers when students are habitually late to classes that follow rehearsals.

Remember that while an excellent opening is essential, the closing is even more important. If you have your players in the palm of your hand at the end of each rehearsal, they are not apt to wander by the next day.

Chapter 8

Conducting
the All-Important String Rehearsals

In much orchestral literature the strings have the most to do and very often have the most difficult parts. Therefore, string sectional rehearsals are very important. There is always a way to work these into the schedule, at least in schools today which do not adhere to as rigid scheduling as they did years ago.

When I was in high school, we had full orchestra rehearsal every day, and the only contacts we had with string literature were before- or after-school ensemble rehearsals, attending live concerts, and listening to the radio. (We didn't have TV, but there were radio concerts.) Many of us went to college and "caught up" there, especially those who majored in music. This is one reason that I favor a schedule in which string rehearsals are held three days per week and full orchestra two. Many of my former students have told me that when they went to college they seemed to have a better background in string literature and the refinements of string playing than some of the other students.

In your preparation for string rehearsals you must, of course, know the string parts well and know how they fit into the entire composition. Straight string selections may not be as intricate as full orchestra numbers, but they may have tricky sections and many subtleties to work out. Don't neglect them in your preparation. All difficult spots (fingering and bowing) should be marked in pencil, as sometimes another way might work out better. Many times the bowings must be changed since students cannot yet use the professional bowings printed in the music.

Observations have revealed that sometimes a string specialist will concentrate heavily on the string section at the expense of the others. This should be avoided. Also, a violin (or other string) specialist should not overlook the importance of the rest of the string section. If not too well-prepared on the other instruments, the director should take some instruction in order to be aware of the specific problems of each. This is also true of the instruments in the other sections; a string specialist should have a "speaking acquaintance" with the woodwinds, brass, and percussion.

PURPOSES OF STRING REHEARSALS

String rehearsals serve as technique builders. Also, it is here that you can take time to bring refinement to your orchestral group, whether or not you are a string specialist. It is the strings that give the orchestra its lush sound, with the other sections providing the beauty of color and contrast, as well as precision.

The string rehearsal will also afford time for work on string literature. As mentioned before, it is very important that all string players become acquainted with as much string music as possible in order to learn to execute the various styles and to appreciate the sound that is unique to the string family.

Advance rehearsal of the strings on any composition in which their parts are quite difficult will make full orchestra rehearsals easier. With the string players a bit familiar with the music, you can give adequate attention to the other sections. This does not always have to be done; sometimes you will want the entire group to hear the overall sound of a new selection as they sight-read it.

HELPFUL SUGGESTIONS
FOR THE NON-STRING DIRECTOR

Often the band and orchestra are directed by the same person who is, in essence, a wind or vocal specialist. Probably he will have been exposed to the string instruments, in a limited way, during the course of his college education. Unfortunately, there is time in these courses to cover only the fundamentals, i.e., simple fingerings and bowings. If such a director can avail himself of some individual string instruction, he can benefit greatly.

Many outstanding high school orchestras are directed by non-string specialists. I can cite two specific examples that will testify to this fact.

Mr. Raymond Clithero, the orchestra director at R. A. Long High School, Longview, Washington, is a woodwind specialist; an excellent bassoonist. During his college training, he had some basic string instruction, enough for teaching beginners (which he also does).

He is first bassoonist in the Southwest Washington Civic Symphony which I conducted when he began teaching in Washington. He immediately began asking questions and observing our string rehearsals whenever possible. The concertmaster (who is orchestra director at the other local high school) and I answered his questions and assisted with some fingering and bowing suggestions on occasion. A teacher aide, who is a private violin teacher and assistant concertmaster of the symphony, is assigned to the junior high orchestra and also assists with the senior high at times.

Mr Clithero's predecessors, Mr. William Watson and I, were both string specialists. The standards in the string section have been maintained by Mr. Clithero's fine musicianship and his efforts to add to his knowledge by arranging for assistance when needed.

The second case involves an orchestra that I had the privilege of hearing at the Northwest Division Convention of the Music Educators National Conference in Portland, Oregon in 1965. The group was the Missoula County High School Orchestra, made up of students enrolled in Hellgate and Sentinel High Schools in Missoula, Montana. The director, Mr. Harold Herbig, is also a woodwind specialist, a fine oboist. The program was all exceptionally well done, Mozart's *Konzertantes Quartett* for oboe, clarinet, horn, and bassoon and orchestra attracted my attention in particular. Not only were the four soloists outstanding, but the accompaniment was performed beautifully in accurate style.

In talking with Mr. Herbig, I learned that he has had some fundamental string instruction in college, plus some private work as well. However, he states that he is not a performer on any string instrument, but has mastered the basic elements of bowing and fingering and some position work. He has some assistance from colleagues at the University of Montana, namely, members of the University String Quartet. Many of the members of the orchestra take private lessons from members of this quartet.

So here are two prime examples of what can be done with a good background in music plus knowing where help is available if needed.

Following are several string terms and facts that can be of help to a director who is not a string specialist:

Bowing Terms

Frog: end of bow held by player (also called nut)
Tip: pointed end of the bow (also called point)
Down-bow: (⊓) playing from frog to tip (may start at any spot and pull bow toward tip)
Up-bow: (∨) playing from tip to frog (may start at any spot and move bow toward frog)

Bow markings and terminology are sometimes confusing; this is why it is essential that you know the style of the period in which a composition was written.

Basically there are three types of bow strokes: legato, staccato, and spiccato. All others are modifications of these.

1. *Legato*: smooth, sustained stroke for long or slurred notes. When changing the bow stroke, the wrist is the key to smoothness. The arm motion stops, but the wrist moves on and executes the return bow, The wrist must be well-controlled, but flexible. Practicing long bows for a few moments each day will pay off. (The return bow made at the frog is more difficult, since the pressure on the bow should be gradually released the nearer one gets to the frog). These exercises can be done on open strings or on scale passages for variety.

2. *Détaché*: general term for notes played in separate bows. If accented, they should be sharply detached and played with broad, vigorous strokes.

3. *Martelé* or *Martellato*: "hammered." Separated down-up bows, played on the string with swift strokes and a definite stop between notes. This is usually executed from about the middle to the tip, but may also be performed at the frog for more power. In fast passages the bow can't be stopped between the notes. They should be played detached, but not staccato. In soft passages there is still the separation but not the "hammering" of the sharp attack and not as much bow used. This is the type of bowing used in baroque music, and requires much practice to develop the proper wrist and forearm movement. Some editions of music indicate this by a dot and some by a pointed dash or wedge. The accent mark is also sometimes used, and in some music there are no markings; there is no uniformity. Again, it is necessary to be aware of the style of the period.

4. *Staccato*: specifically a series of martelé notes in the same bow stroke, but generally any short, crisp notes with a break between. The bow is kept on the string, pressure is applied, then immediately released. The dot is the usual indication of this, but the wedge is also sometimes used for very forceful staccato. Some staccato is played with a very short break between the notes:

5. *Portato*: a semi-staccato in which the notes are slurred but slightly detached, accomplished by changes in bow pressure. Indicated:

Figure 8-1

6. *Spiccato* (bouncing bow): executed near the middle of the bow. No two bows being exactly the same, the player will have to determine the right spot. The bow should be held lightly, yet be controlled, and the wrist must be flexible. Practicing down- and up-bows bounced as near to the string as possible at a slow tempo is a good exercise. Gradually the tempo may be stepped up and the stroke shortened. Another way is to start with short, detached, sharply attacked strokes *on the string*, using a flat bow. As the speed is increased and the amount of bow decreased, it should begin to bounce, and the student can then practice control of the bounce. Students should be made aware of the fact that this doesn't happen all at once. Long sessions occasionally don't accomplish as much as spending less time, but working on it each day. Dots under or over notes can indicate staccato or spiccato, but a fast tempo calls for the latter.

Figure 8-2

A passage of eighth note accompaniments in music of the classical or early romantic period is always played spiccato (unless marked "nonspiccato" or "senza spiccato"). Artificial (slow to moderate tempo) spiccato is executed closer to the frog and involves the arm in lifting each stroke. If a very light tone is required, this too can be played nearer the middle of the bow. This is also called bouncing staccato.

7. *Saltando* or *saltato* (French-*sautillé*): "leaping" or "jumping." Here the bow is thrown on the string so that it bounces as required for eighths, sixteenths, or triplets. This type of bowing is useful at a tempo that would be too difficult to execute by conventional spiccato. These notes are usually played with a down-bow, even on a pick-up beat, as it is almost impossible to do it the other way. A prime example of this is in the Finale from the *William Tell Overture* (Figure 8-3).

Figure 8-3

Flying staccato is a series of up-bow spiccatos; light bow pressure using a staccato motion allows the bow to bounce slightly after each note. Ricochet bowing is a series of down-bow spiccatos from a thrown stroke. The foregoing bow techniques are quite difficult and are not encountered very often in high school orchestra music. There are some instances in which they can be used to advantage, and the students should be aware of how and when they can be utilized.

8. *A punta d'arco*: with the point or tip of the bow.

9. *Col legno*: "with the wood": played with the wooden part of the bow rather than the hair. The player tips the bow stick toward him and bounces it on the string. Used occasionally for special effects and to add color to a work.

10. *Ponticello* or *sul ponticello* (French *au chevalet* or *sur le chevalet*; German-*am steg*): "on the bridge." Play near the bridge, creating a rather glassy sound.

11. *Sul tasto* or *sulla tastiera* (French-*sur la touche*; German-*am Griffbrett*): "on the fingerboard." Play near, or actually above, the fingerboard, producing a sort of dreamy effect.

12. *Modo ordinario*: "in the ordinary way." Cancels any of the above special effects.

13. *Tremolo*: rapid up and down movements of the bow, indicated: (♪). (Sul ponticello is often played tremolo for a mysterious

effect.) Played near the tip of bow if soft, nearer the middle if loud. Can also be played on two notes, with a movement of the bow on each:(🎵).

14. *Repeated notes*: often orchestral music contains a series of repeated notes as in Figure 8-4. Such passages should be played in the middle

Figure 8-4

or upper third of the bow, depending upon the volume needed. A slight accent on each down-bow will help keep the passage clear.

15. *Sixteenth notes*: in rapid passages use the middle and upper part of bow. If *ff* use flat bow and lots of movement and pressure (see Figure 8-5).

Schubert: *Symphony No. 8 in B Minor*

Figure 8-5

Down-Up-Bow Techniques

In certain selections successive down-bows are indicated to secure power and accent (Figure 8-6).

Beethoven: *Egmont Overture*

Figure 8-6

They can be harsh and scratchy if not careful. Practice these often, being sure to have the bow on the string before starting the stroke each time.

Chords are very often played with successive down-bows also. The same sort of practice applies here (Figure 8-7).

Figure 8-7

Students may tell you that they see professional players on TV or in person who do not always have the bow on the string before starting their notes or chords. Your answer can be that they have perfect control of the bow and are able to play smoothly the moment it touches the string. This has been acquired through years of work on bow techniques in the manner in which they themselves are now practicing. Also, professionals have much better instruments and bows than most students, which insures less scratching.

As much as possible, down-bows are used on accented beats and up-bows on the unaccented ones. However, there are many exceptions, and sometimes the reverse is done for certain effects (especially by professionals). The following two illustrations show how bowings are indicated so that the heavily accented beat will be on the down-bow (Figure 8-8 and Figure 8-9).

Figure 8-8

Figure 8-9

In Figure 8-8 the two notes marked with dots in the first measure should be played staccato (on the string), since it is not a fast tempo and marked *f*. This gives a fairly strong sound. In Figure 8-9 the notes indicated to be played short should be spiccato because it is in a faster tempo and is a classical work that is fairly light in character. This passage can be bowed two ways: I prefer to start the first measure up-bow (it is not heavily accented, since it is marked *p*); then the slurred spiccatos will come on the up-bow. The succeeding bowings taken as they come will result in the heavily accented first beat of the eighth measure being played down-bow. If the passage is started down-bow, it should be done from the middle to the tip and the bow must be stopped before playing the three eighth notes in the second measure.

In a passage such as the following, the marked bowing is necessary for students (especially in duple time and a fast tempo) (Figure 8-10).

Figure 8-10

If they try to play them in separate bows (as some professionals do), the passage usually ends in sounding as if it were written as in Figure 8-11. Or else the sixteenth note is stressed too much.

Figure 8-11

However, in ¾ meter the bowing doesn't come out right in a series of dotted eighths and sixteenths, and the wrong beats are likely to be accented. Therefore, they do have to be played with separate bows at times, and this type of practice should be included in drills.

¾ meter presents other bowing problems many times, because if the bowing is done as it comes, three quarter notes throw it out of balance and the up-bow comes on the accented beat. This can be overcome by taking two notes in one bow with a slight break between them (Figure 8-12).

Figure 8-12

Another problem is also solved with the bowing shown in Figure 8-12. If taken in separate bows, the tendency would be to play the dotted quarter and eighth (in the second bar) with the same amount of bow, putting too much emphasis on the shorter note.

If the second violins and violas have an accompanying figure such as the following, there are three ways it can be played. (See Figure 8-13.)

Figure 8-13

This occurs in most waltzes and in some other types of music also. If the passage is very delicate, a light spiccato is more graceful than short strokes on the string. In a rather vigorous part, the bow can be kept on the string and rather broad strokes used. In a Viennese waltz there is sometimes a slight accent on the second beat, and the first bowing is preferable, especially for young players. I have experimented with the three bowings and usually have players use the first. Professionals can be observed using any of the three methods, and so it is largely up to the conductor. Sometimes it takes a lot of patience to get the effect you desire. Young players usually use too much bow and pressure to get a very delicate sound, and it requires much practice.

A similar figure also needing the same type of work is afterbeats. (Figure 8-14.)

Figure 8-14

When playing delicate passages, a small amount of bow is used and it is lifted on the rests. Playing them all up-bow gives a lilting effect. More brisk passages can be bowed down-up with the bow just stopped during the rests. At times very accented afterbeats are called for, and are played all down-bows.

Additional Relevant Terms

1. *Double stops*: playing notes on two strings at the same time. Thirds, sixths, and octaves are the most common. Usually these are played *divisi* in high school orchestras; the outside players taking the higher notes. The intonation often suffers if all the players attempt them.

2. *Chords*: many times chords of three or four notes are called for. If they are not too difficult (some open strings included), all the players can play them. (Be sure all strings are in tune before starting a selection in which there are many open string parts.) For better intonation and increased volume, any difficult chords should be divided.

3. *Corda* (French-*corde*; German-*Saite*): string.

4. *Sul*: "on." Sul G-play passage on G string.

5. *Sordino* (French-*sourdine*; German-*Dämpher*): mute.

6. *Senza*: "without," e.g., senza sordino, etc.

7. *Vibrato*: vibrating the tone with an oscillating movement of the left hand. Used quite consistently by string players on notes of sufficient duration. By the time they are in high school, players are usually using vibrato, but most have not fully mastered it. Drills on long tones with concentration on vibrato should be conducted often. Sometimes "non vibrato" or "senza vibrato" is indicated where a composer wishes a more bland tone.

8. *Ripieno:* "full." Used especially in the *concerto grosso* of the baroque period to indicate that the entire orchestra should play.

9. *Senza ripieni*: first desks only of orchestra play.

10. *Fingered tremolo*: rapid back and forth fingering using slurred bow strokes. Indicated: (♪).

11. *Portamento*: "carrying." Gliding from one tone to the next. (Do not confuse this term with *portato*.) This can be very effective if not overdone. Sometimes a glide ending on a harmonic is impressive. It may be indicated in the music as shown in Figure 8-15.

Figure 8-15

12. *Glissando*: similar to *portamento*, usually a long, more pronounced slide up or down the string. May be marked *gliss* with an oblique line between the two notes that begin and end the glide. (The line may be either straight or wavy.) (Figure 8-16.)

Figure 8-16

13. *Pizzicato*: plucking the strings. Can be done with the left hand for certain effects, but usually the first and/or second fingers of the right hand are used. Left hand pizzicato is usually indicated with a + above the notes to be plucked (with or without the word *pizz.*). *Arco* means to return to using the bow.

14. *Harmonics* (French-*sons harmoniques*; German-*Flageolett-Töne*; Italian-*flautato, flautando*): soft, high tones produced by lightly touching the string at one of its fractional points. Indicated by a circle above the note. Artificial or fingered harmonics are produced by stopping the string with a finger and touching it lightly a fourth higher. The sound heard is two octaves above the stopped note. The note to be fingered is written as an ordinary note and the one to be lightly touched as a diamond-shaped note. Sometimes the actual pitch is also written. (See Figure 8-17.) A harmonic a twelfth

Figure 8-17

higher than the stopped note can also be produced by touching the string lightly a fifth higher. These are rarely called for in orchestral music. Artificial harmonics are written very infrequently for cello and bass.

15. *Flautando*: "like a flute." In addition to being a direction to play harmonics, this term is also used in the same sense as *sul tasto*, to play near or above the fingerboard.

KEY PRINCIPLES OF GOOD STRING PERFORMANCE

Being a string player, I am indebted to my private teachers and a professor at the University of Washington for my understanding of the fundamental principles of good string playing. Each of the following points should be given attention during rehearsals, but especially in string rehearsals:

1. For soft passages:
   a) Use upper part of bow.
   b) Play near fingerboard.
   c) Turn stick of bow toward fingerboard, using less hair.
   d) Use little bow pressure.
   e) Use slow bow unless tremolo or other fast notes are indicated (then use small amount of bow).
2. For loud passages:
   a) Use lower part of bow unless long sweeping strokes are indicated.
   b) Play away from the fingerboard, nearer the bridge.
   c) Play with flat bow.
   d) Use much bow pressure.
   e) Use fast bow.
3. For *crescendo*, up-bow is preferred.
4. For *decrescendo*, down-bow is preferred. (Be able to do the opposite of 3 and 4; sometimes it just works out that way.)
5. Use down-bow on accents, if possible.
6. Usually use up-bow on unaccented beats and pickups.
7. Change bow without undue accenting.
8. Place bow on the string before playing. (7 and 8 help eliminate some of the unmusical sounds that string players produce if not careful.)
9. Shift finger position on the accent and/or on the change of bow, if possible.
10. For speed use middle part of bow (unless very soft).
11. Use tip or near tip for tremolo.
12. Don't linger on open strings unless a specific effect is called for. The open E on the violin is especially shrill. Using them in fast passages is not too noticeable and facilitates the execution.
13. For precision for the most part, all bowings should be identical for all players in each section. However, for certain effects bowings can be altered. For instance, half the section may play a passage slurred and half separated bows. This is done in cases where a fairly heavy tone is required but the effect should be smooth and not choppy. Also, in some instances half a section will play pizzicato and half arco; in this way a pizzicato sound is obtained, but with more

volume. On occasion conductors have players change bows at different times in a sustained passage, similar to the "staggered" breathing sometimes done by choral groups.

14. Care of instrument and bow: Players should always have a soft cloth in cases (changed periodically) with which to wipe rosin off the instrument and strings and also off the bow stick after playing a selection in which *col legno* bowing is used (the hair of the bow should not be touched with a cloth or fingers). The tension on the bow should always be loosened when it is not in use.

MAKING STRING REHEARSALS WORTHWHILE

At first string rehearsals will appeal to the players. After a time, going over difficult spots in the full orchestra music tends to lose its punch. The amount of time you can spend on string literature depends, of course, on the schedule; it is very worthwhile to be able to explore at least a minimum number of string selections and work them up to performance level.

The suggestions for successful full orchestra rehearsals also apply to sectionals, i.e., keeping the rehearsal interesting and moving right along, use of the chalkboard, variety in the music, etc. To finish the period with some interesting string selection will do much to make the entire period an effective one. The players will leave with a more satisfied feeling than if they finish with a fragmented number. This can't always be done, I know, as the full orchestra numbers may need to be drilled upon until the last moment when preparing for a performance.

Following are 15 things to do in order to accomplish your purposes in string rehearsals:

1. Run through particularly difficult string parts of full orchestra numbers prior to full rehearsal (at least some of the time).
2. Rehearse slowly at first, paying attention to all the elements of the music, i.e., intonation, rhythm, dynamics, etc.
3. Experiment with various bowings if the markings used do not bring about the desired results.
4. Try different positions for specific tone quality or ease of execution. (Playing a passage on one string or another will produce a different effect.)
5. Work on balance within the section. Without the other sections present this will be an easier task.
6. Make use of the chalkboard for the schedule and to clarify a passage or technique.
7. If you are a string player, demonstrate by playing a passage. Where this is not possible, perhaps the concertmaster or other first chair person can assist.

8. Build technique through scales and finger and bowing patterns.
9. Work on dynamics and sustaining of tone, especially near the tip of the bow.
10. Explain and work on various string styles in music of different periods.
11. Always be alert to developing tone quality and judicious use of vibrato.
12. At times the strings can be divided into two sections, using a student assistant or teacher aide for one. This can be useful if two sections have the same figuration, such as in Figures 8-18 and 8-19.

Mendelssohn: *Fingal's Cave Overture*

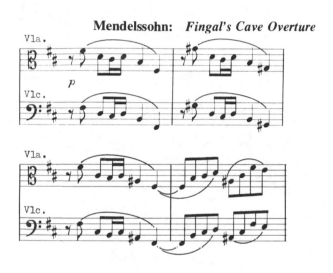

Figure 8-18

Mendelssohn: *Fingal's Cave Overture*

Figure 8-19

13. Many times concentrated work must be done with the inner parts, i.e., second violins and violas. They can be weak and fail to support the melodic line, or not be heard if they have an important part such as in Figure 8-20.

Figure 8-20

14. Give ample attention to the bass line, for therein lies the entire support of the section. Intonation in cello and bass parts is very important, especially if they play in octaves. Any slight discrepancy is very noticeable. (Figure 8-21.)

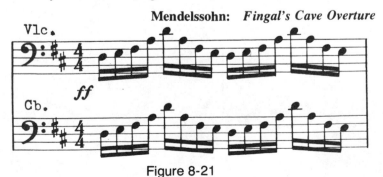

Figure 8-21

Figure 8-21 (continued)

15. Sometimes it is necessary to work with one group, say the second violins, on difficult passages. This can be done near the end of the period and the others excused to study in practice rooms or study area, if the school has one. (They can also practice in the practice rooms.) The group rehearsing can be divided to work out a particularly hard part. It is a good idea to have a few of the weaker players play with stronger ones rather than by themselves. It will be less embarrassing for them and they will gain confidence; they also may be spurred on to practice more on their own.

RECOMMENDED STRING REPERTOIRE

Following is a partial list of string selections I have used. These have been chosen because they represent the various musical periods and will enhance the understanding of different styles. Also, they vary in the degree of difficulty. Some can be worked up rather quickly, offering a feeling of success; others will take longer and be more of a challenge. As well as being interesting, they present many of the rhythmical, bowing, and fingering problems discussed in this chapter and elsewhere:

Adagio for Strings - Barber
Brandenburg Concertos #3 in G Major and #6 in B Flat Major - Bach
Concerto in G Minor - Scarlatti
Concerto Grosso with Piano Obbligato - Bloch
Concerto Grosso Op. 6, No. 2 - Handel
Concerto Grosso Op. 3, No. 8 - Vivaldi
Concerti Grossi Op. 6, Nos. 1-12 - Corelli
Death of Ase and Anitra's Dance from *Peer Gynt* - Grieg
Eine Kleine Nachtmusik - Mozart
Liebeslieder Waltzes - Brahms
Minuet - Boccherini
Minuet - Bolzoni

Nocturne for Strings - Faure
Octet for Strings - Mendelssohn
Overture for Strings - Jacob
Passacaglia and Fugue - Graves
Perpetual Motion - Bohm
Quartet in F Major - Stamitz
St. Paul's Suite - Holst
Serenade - Elgar
Serenade for Strings - Tschaikowsky
Simple Symphony - Britten

Chapter 9

Coping with Personnel and
Discipline Problems During the Rehearsal

You, as a music director, are not dealing with just notes, rhythm, tonal blend, and other technical considerations, but with students, administrators, parents, and townspeople as well. At times situations will arise that no musical background or training will solve. In dealing with these "people" problems, you have to have self-confidence and assurance, and be able to make decisions and stand by them. Care must be taken, however, that self-confidence does not evolve into pomposity; a pompous director will only evoke ridicule, not genuine respect. You must be understanding and realize that any problems that come up are quite real to the persons involved.

This chapter contains suggestions and techniques for dealing with people problems. Inasmuch as most of them occur during rehearsals, that is the time to do something about them. (I cannot recall any disciplinary problems occurring at performance time.) You can't afford to lose precious rehearsal time because of disruptive incidents that cause inattention; if a couple of words fail to halt a disturbance, the person causing the trouble may have to be asked to leave so that you can go on; a conference about the matter can be held later. Unless you decide that in certain cases ignoring immature behavior for a time might help the situation, these matters should be dealt with promptly in order to have effective rehearsals.

UTILIZING AUTHORITY EFFECTIVELY

To command attention and respect without being a complete authoritarian should be an important part of your rehearsal technique. The players must recognize that you are "in charge" in this group in which everyone must work together as a unit. Musical efficiency and fair play are quickly recognized by students; therefore, a sound musical background and an understanding of human nature on your part will go far in gaining the cooperation of the group. Becoming a successful music director takes an enormous amount of energy, enthusiasm, musicianship, diplomacy, patience, and a sense of humor; in return, there are many moments of glorious gratification.

SOME RESOURCES AVAILABLE

Inevitably, problems will present themselves; some will be easily settled and some will call for delicate handling. You can rely on your past experiences to some extent in taking care of certain situations; sometimes talking with a colleague or counselor in the school might be of help. If a student has problems elsewhere, the counselor most likely will have such information in his folder. An examination of this might give you a clue as to the cause of the problem as well as some insight into how other teachers have handled the student.

Discussion about common problems with colleagues in school or at meetings can be helpful. If a student with whom you have had a bit of difficulty transfers to another school, informing your colleague about the situation and what you did about it can be very useful to him. Of course, these circumstances can be reversed, and any information you receive can be helpful to you. As is sometimes said, "two heads are better than one."

COMMON PROBLEMS
AND HOW TO SOLVE THEM

While it is impossible to know exactly just what types of situations might develop, you can be aware of some kinds of problems common to high school students that, if not resolved, can affect rehearsals and the morale of the group.

Dissatisfaction With the Seating

Sometimes students feel that they should be in a different position in the section; sometimes it is the parents who are most disturbed. On one occasion I was faced with this situation—the parents were not satisfied with the chair their child occupied. Seating had been arranged via challenge; the students had voted and I had concurred. I refused to make any changes, and in time the parents accepted the fact that the students sitting ahead deserved to be there. Perhaps they were not happy about it, but they acquiesced and the student remained in the group and seemed satisfied. Strangely enough, in later years this person has been more directly involved in music than the others who were ahead in the orchestra.

Sometimes a parent or a private teacher will request that his child or student be placed without challenge. This, of course, should not be done if the others are required to try out in some way. The only exception should be in the case of someone who is obviously far ahead of the others and it is a unanimous vote of the students that he or she be placed ahead. If a student drops from orchestra because of your adherence to the rules, not much is lost; in fact much is gained—good rapport with the group.

Criticism of Duty Assignments

Students may feel that favoritism is being shown in appointments to various duties. Care must be exercised that the same people are not selected too many times. Holding elections for the major positions is often done, and this is satisfactory. However, with minor or one-time-only duties, asking for volunteers and then making selections is a good method. Attempt to involve different people at different times. Knowing how busy you are and how easy it is to forget who did what, I recommend keeping a record of these duty assignments as a precaution against causing a feeling of unfairness among the students. It may seem to be just one more thing to keep track of in your busy schedule, but these things are important to young people at this age, and they will respect you for your fairness and organization.

Sometimes problems arise that you have no way of anticipating. This type of situation occurred once in my experience. The students had decided that the position of librarian(s) should be a volunteer job. This particular year I selected two girls from several volunteers. Since the job consisted of stamping, marking, filing, mending, and passing out and collecting music, they would be working together. They played in different sections of the orchestra, and I was not aware of the fact that they had a personality clash and disliked each other very much. They managed to keep this hidden during rehearsals and concerts by not associating with each other. However, when they realized that they would have to work together, each came to me separately and asked to be excused or to have another responsibility. I called both parties together and told them I would honor their requests. I asked which one would like to remain on as librarian, and one was decided upon. I asked her if she would like to select her own co-worker from among the other volunteers, which she did. I thanked them for bringing this to my attention so that a solution could be worked out and a conflicting situation averted. From this I learned how to avoid this type of problem. After that I appointed only one librarian, and if a co-worker was desired, the librarian did the selecting.

How To Deal With Unruliness

Discipline problems may arise from time to time for various reasons. One cause can be idleness. Working with one section of the orchestra for more than a few minutes while the rest do nothing can lead to trouble, i.e., talking, playing or tuning instruments, moving chairs, stands, or music about, all of which can cause distractions.

Sometimes part or all of the group members can be affected by something that occurred in a previous class or at home, a happening involving students or the school in some way, or even the world situation. I have always made it a point to try to ascertain the cause of the problem rather than concentrating on the problem itself only. A few well-chosen words can help settle the students if something has happened that affects everyone. Sometimes letting them know you understand their feelings will make it easier for them to cope with a problem.

Usually personnel or discipline problems of any magnitude should be settled privately, if at all possible. Something said right at the moment can sometimes save a situation and no more need be done, depending on the seriousness of the matter. The student should not, at least on the first offense, be sent to the principal's office. This is passing the buck, and means that you are unable to cope with the problem. This can cause loss of the confidence of the group. The student who is causing the disturbance can be asked to go to a practice room and practice and meet with you after class. This removes the disturbance and allows for a private meeting. Unless it is the last period in the day or he has a study period following orchestra, the meeting will have to be short. At least you can get a bit of an idea about what may be bothering the student, and arrange for a talk later to discuss how it can be settled.

The private meeting should be a friendly chat. Questions can be posed that may reveal the cause of the behavior. Perhaps you made a remark that was misunderstood by the student. Maybe he is not feeling very well. Sometimes the student's responsibilities to the group need repeating. A few of the more immature students may make a bid for attention; a knowledge of their background can help in handling some situations. Rarely does a disciplinary problem arise that cannot be solved through sympathetic discussion. However, it does happen occasionally that more stern action need be taken; two incidents in my own experience come to mind.

Disruptive Behavior

One of my students was very good at creating minor disturbances by flighty, impulsive behavior. At times these disruptions became rather major, and I spoke out right at the moment. We had some talks, but this didn't seem to cure the problem. After inquiring about him and examining background material, I found that he had been attempting to secure attention throughout all his school years. The section leader had a talk with him, pointing out the responsibilities everyone has in a group situation such as orchestra. A student committee also tried to deal with him, and some of them were all for "kicking him out," but we decided to try ignoring his childishness and to ask if he would help the librarian with his duties (after getting the okay from the librarian). Gradually, he perceived that his antics were not being noticed, and he gained some attention through other means (the responsibility of assisting the librarian plus increased competence on his instrument). The episodes became fewer and fewer. I hope that this helped him over a troublesome period and assisted him in gaining a mature perspective for later life.

Duties Can Be Assets

I have found that encouraging students to volunteer for duties connected with the smooth operation of the orchestra helps them learn responsibility and gives them a bit of insight as to all that goes into a group of this type. In the case of a student with attention problems such as the above, having some responsibility can increase his self-esteem and keep him busy enough to help get rid of excess energy and frustrations. Sometimes students of this type may be very talented and sensitive and are good potential musicians (even conductors). If their energies are channeled in a positive direction, you may become very proud of them.

Excessive Egotism

One year, two wind players who came to my orchestra from the band (the two groups rehearsed simultaneously) caused a problem. They were the best players on their instruments in the school, and they knew it. They reasoned that they could do just about as they pleased and no one would call them on anything because of who they were. After repeatedly arriving late, interrupting the rehearsal by talking and laughing (when nothing was funny), missing cues, and in general being very obnoxious and ignoring my rather forceful requests for improving their behavior, they were called in for a conference. The students couldn't get through to them and neither could I, and in this case there were no regular duties to assign since they were carried out by the string players who were there every day.

After talking with the band director who said that they were also exhibiting rather cocky behavior in band at times, we decided to give them three chances to correct their behavior or they would be out of orchestra. They must have felt that this was an idle threat, and that I needed them so badly that I wouldn't let them go. They were mistaken, subsequently dismissed, and two others taken in to replace them. These two were not as experienced nor as competent, but they regarded being chosen as an honor and worked very hard in order to meet the standards. They were attentive and orderly and the whole orchestra settled down.

The other two were quite subdued by the action taken, but there was never any protest from them nor anyone else since everyone knew that they had been given enough chances and they "had it coming." At the beginning of the next semester they came to me and asked if they could be reinstated. I declined, since the other two had worked out satisfactorily and I felt that this was a good lesson in group responsibility for everyone. This happened many years ago, and I don't know whether the story was told to new students or not, but it never happened again.

Coping with Outside Requests Courteously

Sometimes things are asked of a musical director from outside sources. Some of these are things one might wish to do and others are not. I have learned to follow these guidelines when requests are presented:
1. Consider each request carefully
    a) Could there be possible complications?
    b) What are the educational values?
    c) How will it fit into the schedule?
    d) Is this a one-time affair or could it become repetitious?
    e) Will it involve travel and/or expense?
    f) Could it cause personnel problems?
2. Discuss any unusual or travel request with the administration
3, Obtain requests in writing to avoid misunderstanding
4. Give a decision as soon as possible
5. Don't hesitate to deny the request if it appears unreasonable
6. Give a realistic explanation if the request is denied

When I was beginning my career as an orchestra director, I was surprised by several calls from local private music teachers asking if it would be possible to have one or more of their students rehearse concertos with the orchestra. This would be a wonderful experience for them, they said. Since I hadn't given this sort of thing any thought ahead of time, I hedged and said I would think about it. After several such requests, I made up my mind to say no. I reasoned that receiving such "guests" would not be without difficulties, since I didn't know where I could draw the line. I absolutely didn't have the rehearsal time to accommodate very many such students, and if I agreed to take a student of one teacher, others would be unhappy if I didn't give the same consideration to their students. Another point was: who would buy all the orchestrations? The school budget was rather lean and even renting very many such orchestrations would get expensive.

Right then I made a rule that I never broke: if a student was a regular member of the orchestra and was competent enough to play a movement of a concerto at a performance, he could be considered for this. Some of the piano teachers were a bit unhappy about this since we didn't use many piano students in orchestra; however, they understood my situation, for the most part, and we have enjoyed many years of cooperation in the interest of music.

Several times we have had student soloists appear with the orchestra, among them one pianist who played the piano parts (when required) and also played tympani in the orchestra. After I organized the Southwest Washington Civic Symphony, the tradition of having student soloists at the spring concert was started. High school seniors and college students are now eligible to audition to perform with the symphony.

HOW TO INSURE GOOD ATTENTION

If you keep the entire group attentive throughout the rehearsal, your discipline problems will be very few and far between. A busy, interested, attentive player has no time to make trouble. (There may be an occasional exception such as the aforementioned students, who must be dealt with for the good of the group.)

Following are ten suggestions for helping to hold attention:
1. Start rehearsal on time
2. Be enthusiastic yourself—it's catching!
3. Have enough material on hand to fill the entire period
4. Present different types of music
5. Keep rehearsal moving and interesting
6. Avoid working with one section alone for very long
7. Select compositions in which brass and percussion are not idle for long periods, or arrange for these players to be excused part of the time
8. Do everything you can to insure the students' comfort. If the room is too hot or too cold, they will become restless; also, the instruments will not stay in tune, which is discouraging
9. Compliment whenever possible
10. End on time

HOW PARENTS AND ADMINISTRATORS CAN
HELP DEAL WITH DISCIPLINE PROBLEMS

There may be occasions when parents and/or administrators need to be brought into the picture regarding certain problem situations. I have always felt that exhausting every means possible before enlisting the help of parents or school officials is the way to go. To rely on outsiders very often tends to weaken your position.

When additional assistance is needed, I feel that parents should be called in first. Usually a frank discussion with them alone and then with the student present will resolve most difficulties. If not, then a 4-way conference can be arranged: student, director, parents, and school official. If the problem gets that involved, usually some rather stiff disciplinary action results. Only in rare cases is it necessary to go that far. This is not to say that you should have conferences with parents only when difficulties with their child are evident; it is good to know the parents and to discuss the student's progress and any other pertinent topics from time to time.

There may be an occasional student who is not really very interested in orchestra, but whose parents want him to be there. He may cause problems in order to be suspended or dismissed. A conference should be held to determine just why he wishes out. It may be that he is a bit discouraged because he feels he is not progressing; perhaps private lessons might be an answer. Sometimes sports or other activities are more alluring and he spends all his spare time on these and doesn't practice his music. At times students hit a "plateau" beyond which they don't seem to advance, and get bored with it all. If, despite all your efforts to make it interesting, the student and parents decide it is too much of a struggle, he may drop out. I have had a few such cases, and sometimes after a semester or two they decided they wanted to come back and worked harder than ever to "catch up."

I usually encourage such students who are having problems making progress unless they are real troublemakers or the parents insist they drop out, because I know that sometimes it is regretted. One of my students became quite disinterested and wasn't practicing, and so his parents decided it wasn't worth the effort and he quit. His mother told me later that after he finished college he asked his parents why they hadn't *made* him practice and stay in orchestra as he really did enjoy it. He began practicing again and has found some satisfaction in it, but he missed a lot in his musical development.

In another case, a girl was not working at her music at all and her interest was at a standstill. I talked with her parents also, and we decided to stand pat and encourage her to continue. She had been ill the previous fall and we were sure that her listless attitude was a result of being at a rather low ebb physically. They even continued her private lessons (they could hardly afford it) because they felt that the potential and interest were really there somewhere. She kept at it, protesting a bit, but by the next fall she was "with it" again and eventually gained the ultimate for a violinist: concertmaster.

HOW CAN STUDENTS HELP?

Sometimes the most effective way to solve problems created by students is to have the students themselves work them out. This can be quite satisfactory when done with your supervision and guidance.

A disciplinary committee of first chair people (one from each section, e.g., strings, woodwinds, brass, percussion) can sit in judgment upon members who have caused problems. Students usually don't want their peers criticizing them, as they know that they might be harder on them than adults might be. If a larger committee is desired, the first chair people from all the string sections can be included, since there are more players there than in any other section. The committee can be elected rather than comprised of first chair people only, if desired. You can reserve the right to meet with them and to review their decisions.

Each first chair person can be responsible for the behavior of the people in his or her section, talking with any who might be getting out of line in any way.

Other students can talk privately with the one in question. Their concern for his proper behavior will, in many cases, make him "shape up." Students don't like to lose the friendship of their classmates.

As a rule, not many serious problems come up in a group such as orchestra. Most of the students have developed self-discipline because they have had to practice their instruments in addition to other school work and activities. I have found that many of the people in the music groups are among the busiest in the school—they seem to be able to carry on many things at the same time, and are well-organized. Since orchestra is not a required subject, they are usually there because they want to be and are willing to work and cooperate in order to have the best organization possible.

DEVELOPING PRIDE IN THE GROUP

Pride is one of those intangible things that results from attitudes and circumstances. Students in a performing musical group are in a position similar to those in sports, i.e., much of what they learn is displayed before an audience. True, it is a different type of activity and not so competitive, but receiving a high rating at a music meet is akin to winning a game.

If the students are proud to be members of the orchestra, they will usually do what is necessary in order that the group's reputation be maintained at a high level. Practicing to learn their parts well, being punctual and attentive, helping in whatever capacity they can, and remembering that they represent the school when performing are things they will work on willingly.

How is pride attained? It is rather cumulative, one thing building upon another. The following can be of help:

1. *Successful concerts*. Being well-received at a performance produces self-esteem and is a great morale and pride builder. It has to be understood that much work goes into successful concerts; they don't just "happen." Each person must be alert and perform to the best of his ability.

2. *Establishment of a first-rate reputation.* This includes not only performance, but also conduct and personal responsibility. Such things as politeness and tidiness at a performance site are examples.

3. *Maintaining instruments in tip-top playing condition.* At the first sign of trouble, students should make a point of correcting it. This may vary from a worn clarinet pad to a sticking trumpet valve to the need to rehair a bow. All accessories should be on hand at all times (mutes, extra strings, extra bow if possible, valve oil, etc.), and instruments should be spotless and shiny. This gives the orchestra a neat-looking appearance.

4. *Some uniformity in dress for performances.* This will enhance the feeling of presenting a favorable impression, which in turn increases pride.

5. *Articles in the newspaper.* Some papers have a section on school news once a week, and, of course, the school paper should carry articles on musical activities. Someone in the group can be a reporter.

6. *Accentuate the positive.* Tell them when they make a good appearance and play well. Let them know you are really proud of them.

There is nothing like being asked to perform to make the group members feel proud. The above can all help this come about.

Student Body and Community Pride

It is always hoped that the school student body and staff (as well as the community at large) will take pride in the fact that a fine orchestra exists in the school.

Several years ago a former student, who was then attending a university, told me that a friend in the orchestra there told her how glad she was to be out of high school and in the university since there an orchestra was appreciated. The girl from our city was quite surprised, since she had never felt downgraded by her peers. Her friend said that the majority of students in her high school felt that those people in the orchestra were very "square" and even rather strange. Perhaps this orchestra did not appear often, or maybe the music chosen was difficult for high school students to understand. They may not have presented a very striking appearance, or the orchestra members themselves may have been apologetic and not too enthusiastic. A lot depends on you, the director, in generating enthusiasm and positive attitudes, which in turn produce pride in the group. If the players talk it up in a positive manner, the enthusiasm can be "caught" by others in the school.

I'm sure that there are some students in all high schools who feel that music students are "different" since they themselves have no understanding of music other than what they hear on radio and TV. I know the music instructors in the elementary and junior high schools do their best to instill some appreciation of music in the children as they pass through their classes; however, on some it is lost. One way to build up an interest in orchestra is to have your group perform for the younger children whenever it can be arranged, explaining a bit about the organization and the music that is played. If people learn something about a group, they are more likely to understand and appreciate it, and eventually they will be proud that their school has this organization.

Chapter 10

Performance:
A Climax to Rehearsals

While the fact that an orchestra must be educational cannot be ignored, performances must not be overlooked either. The nature of music is such that it is meant to be performed. Playing for an audience is an experience in poise, remembering what has been learned, and enriching the lives of the listeners as well as those of the performers. It is a fine stimulant for further study and achievement, a climax to weeks of rehearsing, a marvelous morale builder, and a good public relations project.

Your position as a teacher is somewhat more conspicuous than that of others in the educational field whose work is confined mainly to the classroom. The results of your work are subject to scrutiny by school administrators as well as the public. While some administrators are more interested in the music program than others, they all will ''pop their buttons'' as a result of an outstanding program or an encouraging review in the local newspaper.

This chapter will help you prepare effectively for performances. Included are such things as places you can play, how to tell when the orchestra is ready for performing, and ideas on planning interesting programs (with some examples of well-received programs). Other topics dealt with are actual preparations for performances, duties delegated to student assistants, appropriate attire, and some ''don'ts'' to think about.

HOW OFTEN SHOULD YOU PERFORM?

Generally speaking, there should be enough performances to keep up the interest of the group.

A good rule is to plan several appearances each semester, spaced far enough apart so that you have time to prepare new material. Occasionally performances will bunch up in spite of your plan to keep them spaced. If this happens only now and then, there is no reason not to appear, especially if enough numbers are worked up. Sometimes selections can be repeated for different groups.

You should not hesitate to decline invitations to perform if they will create a hardship or take students out of school too often. One solution is to take a "rain check" and offer to appear at a later date. In this manner the performance has only been postponed, not really canceled. You should keep the door open for future invitations; in other words, don't "burn your bridges behind you." However, people in the community should understand that you must have at least two weeks' advance notice when they request a program (more if it is to be of any length). Unless it is early in the fall, you will probably have enough material prepared to present a few numbers. Most of the school concert dates are set far enough ahead so that there is no problem of having to "rush" material (unless you procrastinate preparing).

Where You Can Perform

I have found it a good idea to perform for the school's own student body for the first appearance in the fall. This serves a dual purpose: 1) the student body, instructors, and administrators become aware that the orchestra is there, and 2) it enables the group to get "in the mood" for performing—a test run, so to speak. This does not mean that this can be a slipshod performance or a dress rehearsal for some outside appearance. On the contrary, it should be a well-prepared concert, the best they can do. If they can play well for their friends, they are off to a good start.

In addition to the usual concerts in the school auditorium or gym, there are numerous places you can take the orchestra to perform. A few are: service clubs, dedications, local conventions, tours to nearby high schools or junior highs, and, of course, music meets or contests. You can also apply to have your group appear at the Music Educators State, Regional, and/or National Conventions. Sometimes trips can be arranged during vacation period; these involve a lot of planning and work, but usually the students are very enthusiastic and will work hard toward this goal.

At times an out-of-town club or group of some sort will sponsor an evening concert, and perhaps you might get on television. My orchestra appeared on a TV station in Portland, Oregon (40 miles away), presenting a half-hour program. A TV set was installed in the auditorium of the school and the whole student body was excused to watch and listen to their orchestra perform. It took the orchestra members out of school for a day, but it was an exciting, educational, and rewarding experience for them.

DECIDING WHEN A SELECTION
IS READY FOR PERFORMANCE

Timing is very important in considering performances by your group. If a composition is presented before it is well-prepared, a substandard performance will result. This can undermine the confidence of the players and be reflected in future appearances. On the other hand, if one waits too long and over-rehearses, the performance can be rather bland because the peak was reached earlier and the spark has now left the players. Result: another substandard performance.

One has to remember that the performers may become somewhat nervous when playing in public, especially when relatives and friends are present (even though they are proud to have them in the audience). I have found that sometimes they are less nervous when playing for strangers (such as when on tour) than at home. However, being a little "keyed-up" is not all bad, as it means that they are alert. If they are well-prepared, the nervousness will not usually affect their playing ability. If it does, they need special help in building self-confidence. A well-prepared program should help overcome this nervousness.

Many times performance dates are set up well in advance, and it is up to you to gauge the rehearsals so that the group is "ready" but not "stale." You can be sure that there will be some interferences to rehearsals such as students being excused for various activities, illness, cancellation of part of the period occasionally, holidays, etc. These must be considered when planning programs and the approximate number of rehearsals needed on certain selections. Sometimes you might rehearse several numbers and then decide before the deadline which ones to use. Following are suggestions that can be helpful in deciding how near ready your group is for a performance.

An Effective Test: Can the Group Play Without You?

After spending considerable time rehearsing a selection, you should step back and listen. Let the group play without a leader. Several things will immediately become apparent. Ask yourself:
1. Is the group able to maintain the correct tempo and stay together?
2. Are the players aware of the dynamic markings without your reminders?
3. Is the ensemble balanced?
4. Are the players listening to each other and allowing the melodic line to come through?

5. Can they make their entrances without the help of your cues?
6. Are they able to count without foot-tapping?
7. Can they make changes in tempo quite well, remembering these from past rehearsals? (They may be a bit ragged on this for a moment without your direction.)

By the answers you give to the above you have some indication as to how well-prepared they are.

Playing in Small Groups

There are occasions when it is advisable to divide the orchestra into small groups such as quartets, quintets, or octets. In this way you can pick up weaknesses that may slip by during full rehearsals or even during sectionals. It is more feasible for strings to be divided than for the entire orchestra, although you can do some woodwind and brass passages in this way, if desired. (Many times wind players have solo passages or are one-on-a-part anyway, and sectionals can usually take care of hearing them to good advantage.)

In ensemble playing it is essential that each player give every ounce of attention to all musical matters. He cannot hide within his section or "fake" his playing. String players are likely to try this at times, since they are not individually exposed in the full orchestra to the extent that wind players are. Because of this exposure, wind players are sometimes more conscientious than string players about working on their parts.

If students know that such small groups are to be selected prior to performances, they may work hard in preparation for this. At times I have also used the small groups set-up for grading purposes. A typical method is to have a string quartet plus a bass form a group and play selected passages from the orchestral work being rehearsed, then another group plays, etc. The rest of the string section listens (I do this during string rehearsal time). In this manner you are hearing each player on his own part, yet he is not playing alone as would be the case in a challenge or test. He will probably do better than if playing alone, and it will be easier for you to assess his ability than if he were playing in the full orchestra.

The same procedure can be applied to the other sections of the orchestra if you wish. I have found this a fairer way to grade than by judging all in the large group, since each player can be heard more clearly. Also, musicianship can be closely observed.

Tape Recordings Can Help Decide

With the availability of good tape recorders, another instrument is at your disposal to help ascertain whether or not a selection is nearly ready to be performed. Tape recorders simply do not lie—if there is an error, it will be recorded.

One of the best ways to use the recorder is to tape a certain portion of the work and play it back to the students immediately in order that the material remains fresh in their minds. There is nothing like letting them hear their own mistakes firsthand. They can rehearse the passage then and there and try to correct the errors. When the whole selection has been rehearsed to the point of being quite well-polished, tape the entire composition. Attention should then be focused on all the musical aspects of the performance from the standpoint of the audience. Let the players help decide whether or not they would feel satisfied to present the work at that point and if not, what needs to be done to improve it.

A tape recorder of good quality is important, as is proper placement of microphones to insure adequate pick-up and balance. Stereo taping gives best results.

Playing for Other Groups

Sometimes a mini-concert can be given for another music group in the school, e.g., band, choir, general music class. This gives the group an opportunity to be heard and to find out how the music comes across. In return, perhaps the band or choir will perform for your group when they are preparing for a concert.

Any time you can get some kind of an audience, the students will be "on their toes" and you can judge just how their performance might be affected by a bit of nervousness.

Be Alert for Signs of Loss of Interest

At times a selection will develop very smoothly, yet you feel that it could stand a little extra refinement. This sometimes can be too much and the students will begin to lose interest. They have been on the piece too long and it has become less than exciting to them. At that point it should be presented as soon as possible for an audience. If this is not convenient, put it aside for a while and have a brush-up just prior to its use at the next concert. Signs that indicate a diminishing amount of enthusiasm for a composition should be watched for, and appropriate action taken to counteract such feelings.

HOW TO PLAN AN INTERESTING PROGRAM

Considerable thought must go into making up a program, both from the standpoint of the audience and that of the players. Two main considerations are necessary for a favorable program, variety and order of presentation.

Variety: What Should Be Included

One of the secrets of a successful program for the general public is variety. You must remember that you are not always going to appear before a sophisticated audience of concertgoers who have backgrounds of music appreciation to draw on. You are performing for parents, friends, and people of the community in all walks of life, some who are knowledgeable in music and some who are not. Unless there is some specific reason for presenting it, an entire program of, say, Beethoven or contemporary music would not be very well received. However, having a theme for a program sometimes works out very well. American music in connection with a national or local celebration, different types of dance music from various countries, music based on folk tunes, music for the ballet, and, of course, appropriate music for Christmas concerts are all examples of things that can be performed.

In most of my programs I have included some standard work such as an overture, prelude, toccata, or something in that style, and/or one or two movements of a symphony (or the entire work if it is a classical one no longer than about 20 minutes). The length of the entire concert is a factor in determining how much of a work to use.

Also included should be shorter numbers, some 3-5 minutes in length, and perhaps a string number. Playing too many selections that are rather lengthy tends to make the audience restless and, at times, even noisy. There should be a climatic number; one that will bring the players' enthusiasm to the highest point and have the listeners figuratively on the edges of their seats. Usually this is the final selection. (It is effective also to have a somewhat stirring conclusion to the first half of the program if there is an intermission.) It should be brilliant, full of life and beauty of tone, with some rapid passages; in all, a selection that will display the ability of the young players and be a thrilling experience for everyone.

Many times the orchestra, band, and choir will present a concert together. In this case, of course, fewer selections are needed, but the element of variety should still be present. In playing for students, one or two novelty numbers always go over well, especially with junior high or elementary audiences.

Arranging Selections on the Program Effectively

The order of the numbers on the program is very important and must be given careful thought. Sometimes after rehearsing for a while you may want to switch a couple of items around for one reason or another; they may just fit better that way.

A good rule to go by is that since audiences are most alert in anticipation at the beginning of a concert, the heavier and longer selections should appear there. An intermission should be included unless the program is a fairly short one (such as part of a larger program of a convention, etc.).

Following the intermission the lighter and shorter selections provide contrast to the first part of the program. The last composition can be longer, especially if it is quite stirring. Sometimes you might wish to do a medley from a musical show or something with varied rhythms, orchestration, and moods for a final number.

Below are examples of typical programs that I have presented that were well-received:

I

Overture: Cosi fan tutte	Mozart
Symphony #8 (Unfinished)	Schubert
First Movement	
Slavonic Dance #8	Dvorak
Serenade for Strings in C	Tschaikowsky
(One or two movements)	
Andalucia Suite	Lecuona
Finlandia	Sibelius

II

Toccata	Frescobaldi-Kindler
Symphony #104 (London)	Haydn
Piano Concerto in A Minor	Grieg
First Movement	
Trumpet Voluntary	Purcell
Symphony of Bells	Beckman
Contra Dance in C	Beethoven
Selections from The *King*	Rodgers-Bennett
and I	

III

Overture: Egmont	Beethoven
Concerto Grosso, Op. 3, #8	Vivaldi
for Two Violins and Strings	
Triumphal March from *Sigurd*	Grieg
Jorsalfar	

Three Dances from *Henry the VIII*	German
Waltz from *Billy the Kid*	Copland
Prelude: Die Meistersinger	Wagner

Each of the above programs contains a variety of time-honored music. None is overly lengthy (an intermission was included in each). The players enjoyed the music and were well-prepared. The arrangement of the selections was done in the manner mentioned above. All of these factors contributed to the enthusiastic reception by the audience.

Examining each program, we find:

Program I began with a light, but rapid overture, "showing off," if you will, the woodwind and string sections. I used only the first movement of the *Unfinished Symphony*; of the two, it is easier listening for a general audience and not quite as difficult to play well as the delicate second movement. The *Slavonic Dance* was a pleasant change of tempo from the previous selection. Next came a string number for variety (also, this gave the winds a breathing spell in preparation for the final two selections). The *Andalucia Suite* is a series of short selections, each varying from the others in tempo and mood, making for audience appeal. *Finlandia*, of course, is such a stirring work that it makes a fine ending to a program. An effective rendition is always received with well-deserved applause.

Program II contained music from most of the periods in musical history, beginning with the baroque *Toccata*. The Haydn work, being only around 20 minutes in length, was done in its entirety. The Grieg *Concerto*, a concert favorite, provided a climactic ending to the first part of the program. After intermission we had three rather brief selections of contrasting nature (some people were a bit surprised to find Beethoven wrote something so light and lively). The concluding medley of tunes familiar to many was a satisfying ending.

Program III was also well-balanced for audience appeal, beginning with a rather heavy overture and ending with a dramatic selection. In between, the string number provided variety in the type of composition as well as in instrumentation. The two dance types, from different periods in musical development, showed interesting contrast, and the march was stately and a change from the usual military marches.

Some Cuts Justifiable on Occasion

In some selections you might want to omit a particularly difficult passage or two. Some musicians are opposed to this, but I have always felt that there are many compositions that should be performed but that have just a few very difficult spots, and cutting out these parts does not harm the continuity. Otherwise these selections would have to be excluded and the students would not be exposed to them. To me this is no different from using arrangements. The above *Prelude to Die Meistersinger* is one in which I made a cut; I would venture to say that not ten people in the audience knew it, but everyone would have been aware of the fact that it should not have been attempted had we left in the section that was beyond the students' capabilities at that stage of development.

Importance of the Concluding Selection

Many times professional symphony orchestras program a complete symphony or concerto as a final number. Audiences attending these concerts are usually a bit different from the high school concert audiences, and therefore programming is somewhat different. However, localities vary; large and small city audiences may have diverse tastes, and you have to "get the feel" of your community. Nevertheless, you should not play down to your audiences. Don't be afraid to give them something that may be a little heavier than what they are accustomed to hearing; they may surprise themselves and like it, especially if the students are enthusiastic about it.

It is not a good idea to finish every program you present with exactly the same type of selection. Sometimes it might be something stately and majestic with powerful chords and sustaining tones, or a fast piece with a flourish at the end. A number containing many different effects can be very interesting; one movement of a symphony can be used if not too long. Referring again to the *Meistersinger* number: it was a bit on the heavy side, but with the cut it wasn't overly long and was a very stirring finish.

In addition to the selections on the above programs, a few suggestions for concluding numbers are:

American Salute	Gould
Bacchanale from *Samson* and *Delilah*	Saint-Saëns
Berceuse and Finale from *The Firebird*	Stravinsky
Dances from *The Bartered Bride*	Smetana
Farandole from *L'Arlesienne* Suite No. 2	Bizet
March from *Tannhauser*	Wagner
Polovetsian Dances	Borodin
Selections from *Faust*	Gounod
Symphony No. 1 (4th Movement) (I omit the Introduction)	Brahms

Symphony No. 5 ("New World")	Dvorak
4th Movement	
The Great Gate of Kiev	Moussorgsky
Triumphal March from *Aida*	Verdi

"Pops" Concerts Can Be a Hit

Presenting "Pops" concerts now and then goes over very well with the community. If you do this, you may want to reserve show tune selections for these.

There is a great wealth of material one can use for this type of concert. Here again, I usually begin with an overture that is quite animated, then go into something in a different vein, perhaps a bit quieter. None of the selections should be long (the overture might be the longest). A suite can be included, since most sections are fairly short. As the program progresses, a few special numbers interspersed between the usual things will give the concert "that extra something." Such specials might be:

1. A percussion solo or ensemble
2. One or two Leroy Anderson selections (*Bugler's Holiday* could be one if you have three good trumpeters)
3. Have a vocalist or two sing some of the show tunes if you are including such a medley
5. Latin-American dances (featuring the rhythm section)
6. A pizzicato number
7. Have one whole section stand and play a number with orchestral accompaniment (e.g., *Dance of the Flutes*; violin solo played by all first violins)
8. An unannounced number
9. A novelty selection (perhaps with sound effects)
10. A number with audience participation
11. At least one selection that is program music. Program notes will enhance this, but if not feasible, it is appropriate at a concert of this type to talk a bit and explain what the composer may have had in mind (or be definite if the composer indicated this).

Encores: Yes or No?

Whether or not there need be an encore at any concert is up to you and tradition. Some communities expect it, others do not. Sometimes the type of performance or the time limit can be a factor in deciding about this. If the final selection is of such vitality that an encore would be anticlimactic, it might be best to omit it. If the applause is such that some acknowledgment by the orchestra is necessary, a portion of the final number can be repeated. There is usually a possible starting point for an encore not too far from the end of the selection.

Encores are usually light and perhaps seasonal, e.g., *Sleigh Ride* in December, *Thunder and Lightning Polka* in January, *April Showers* in the spring, etc. If the program itself has been quite vigorous, an encore of rather quiet beauty is effective. At times more than one encore can be used if the orchestra played exceptionally well (and you have them prepared).

I recall one situation in which the orchestra had presented two encores and the audience called for more. The director could have had the house lights turned on and let it go at that, but he came out and had the group play *The Star Spangled Banner*, which brought the audience to its feet. At the conclusion they could do nothing but leave. We never knew whether the orchestra had exhausted its material, or the director felt that two encores were enough and they were beyond the ability to maintain their excellence, or they had intended to end the program in this manner! This procedure should be used sparingly. I would not advocate making a habit of it, especially in the school's own locality. Far better to have another short encore in reserve if you think it might be needed. There are many selections that can be worked up quickly and kept on hand.

When Lighter Music Is Appropriate

Obviously, certain performances will call for less serious music than others. If you are asked to play incidental music between acts of the school play, for instance, usually something light and melodious will fill the bill. Occasionally some selections that might fit in with the theme of the play can be found and used.

Sometimes string orchestras or ensembles are invited to play background music at functions such as teas, fashion shows, receptions, etc. Here, delicate, rather smooth-flowing selections are suitable.

PREPARATIONS FOR ACTUAL PERFORMANCE

There are always certain preparations for each appearance of the orchestra, aside from preparing the music itself. To take care of these matters adequately will help prevent "concert jitters." Since much time and effort have gone into preparing the selections that make up the program, everyone will be anxious that it be presented in the best manner possible. It must be remembered that any performance is a one-time affair; it must go correctly the first time. By doing everything you can to insure a smoothly run performance, both the audience and orchestra members will benefit.

Know Exact Details

Knowing the precise time of performance as well as the date is important. It never hurts to double-check a few days ahead with the person who extended the invitation to perform (unless it is a school function). It is always possible that there has been a change in time, or even date, and you weren't notified. Also, ascertain who is to introduce the group if this is to be done.

Check Site Carefully

If at all possible, the performance site should be checked over ahead of time (if not feasible, arrive in time to check it before setting up). Be sure that there are enough chairs and a place to leave wraps and instrument cases. The latter should not be left lying backstage unless there is no other place, as this can be an accident factor.

Find out about the heat and ventilation. If there are any noisy fans for cooling or heating, perhaps arrangements can be made to have them turned off during the actual playing. Be sure lighting is adequate so that everyone can see his music and see you well. Discovering at the last minute that the lighting is bad can be rather disastrous. Maybe the only thing you can do about it, even if discovered early, is to move the group around a bit, but that may be of some help.

Instructional Sheets Are Very Helpful

It is a good idea to issue instructional sheets to the students in advance, especially if the place of performance is other than the school. Included should be where to meet (with directions, if necessary), time of arrival, dress, and any other information pertinent to the occasion.

Opening Time Must Be Arranged

Arrangements should be made with the custodian to open the auditorium, gym, or wherever the program is to be, at a certain time for the orchestra, should you wish to have a warm-up there. Also, doors should be opened at a designated time for the audience.

Program Order Reminders a Necessity

A copy of the order of selections should be in each folder. (If there are printed programs, these can be used.) The players can arrange their music in order at the final rehearsal before the concert, or at the warm-up if one is held just previous to the performance. Even so, having a copy of the order of the program right in the folder gives them a feeling of security—they know they won't "goof" and start playing the wrong number.

DUTIES TO DELEGATE

Usually the organization has a set of officers whose duties pertaining to the regular daily routine of rehearsals are quite clearly defined. When it comes time for the orchestra to make a public appearance, these people may have certain things to do and there may have to be others to assist also. The delegation of duties must be done well in advance of the time they are to be executed. The instructions can be typed or written out on cards so that nothing will be overlooked. (Having duplicates of these cards to keep in your file in case of loss of originals is a good idea.)

Stage Manager

The stage manager should assist you in checking out the concert site, if possible. He should be at the place of performance in plenty of time to set up the chairs and music stands. (Usually the stands have to be transported from the rehearsal room as few places can supply enough for a large group.) He will probably need an assistant or two if the stands have to be loaded into a truck and then unloaded and carried in. If the manager has worked with you before, he can probably take charge of things adequately; if not, you will have to supervise. I have always been at the site early enough to be sure that everything is set up the way I want it.

Don't forget that arrangements have to be made to get everything back to the rehearsal room after the concert or during the next day.

Librarian

The librarian should see that all the music to be performed is in each folder and that all folders are at the site of the program. This does not mean that he or she has to carry them personally; just see to it that they are all in the receptacle provided for transporting them.

I have always asked the students to leave the folders at school after the final rehearsal so that they can be checked and all transported together. However, on one occasion my oboist wanted to do some last-minute practicing before a contest-festival and took one number out of the folder after school without the knowledge of the librarian. When the folders were being passed out just before we were to perform, it hit her that she had left the music at home. She came to me in a panic, and since we were out of town, there was no hope of getting the music in time even if we switched places with another group. The only thing I could do was let her use my piano-conductor score which contained the solo cues (being familiar with the music, she could anticipate her entrances). I was very glad that I had done my homework well, since I had to conduct from memory. This taught me to caution players against taking any music home just before a performance.

At some affairs, such as contests where one group leaves and another comes in, the players sometimes take their own folders in. However, if the librarian puts the folders out before anyone goes in, they should be put in the center of the music stands *closed*. Even if the folders are not larger than the stands (some are), they might protrude from one side or the other if left open and could be knocked off as the players come in. This can also occur when they go out for intermission and after the concert, so they should close the folders at those times too.

The librarian is usually responsible for collecting the folders and getting them back in the box or whatever is used for carrying them, unless each person is instructed to put his own in for time-saving purposes.

Ticket Sellers and Ushers

If an admission is to be charged, someone must be on hand to sell tickets and take care of the money during the concert. Also, if there are programs for the audience, people should be at the doors to distribute them. You may or may not wish to have ushers to show people to their seats; usually, if seats are not reserved, people tend to prefer finding their own favorite places to sit.

Obviously, the people to take charge of these duties cannot be from the orchestra. Sometimes a school club will provide the service, or students from another musical organization might do it and yours could reciprocate when they have a concert.

GETTING TO THE PERFORMANCE

If a program is held in the school facilities, students are responsible for arranging to be there. This is also true when playing elsewhere in the community. On an out-of-town trip, I usually make arrangements for a bus (or two, if necessary). In this way, it is easy to check that every player is present and then proceed with less tension than if everyone goes in cars (even if driven by parents). Also, students usually enjoy traveling together on such occasions. Of course, an adult supervisor should be on each bus; the driver should be free to give his undivided attention to the driving. Usually you can find a willing parent from the music club or PTA who can be counted on to help.

Another positive aspect of traveling by bus is that the entire group will arrive at the same time; also, there will be fewer vehicles to park.

I recall an instance when my group traveled in cars to an out-of-town concert. Everyone arrived on time except the panel truck with the percussion players and equipment. There were some anxious moments waiting out on the curb, expecting that particular truck to round the corner at any moment. As it happened, it did arrive in time; they had a bit of trouble finding the way. We really had to hurry to set up the equipment in time for the performance. After that incident, I always used buses for out-of-town engagements. Sometimes some of the equipment may have to be transported by other means, it's true, but the other vehicle can stay right behind the bus (or between, if there are two buses).

Planning the Time of Arrival

When to arrive is important. I have always requested that students begin arriving 45 minutes before curtain time, and not later than 30 minutes before. While this may seem unduly early, I cannot overemphasize the importance of being there in plenty of time. Sometimes there may be a problem with an instrument, or something of a different nature might be amiss. The players should have time to warm up their instruments and fingers and to settle down into the frame of mind for performing.

Requesting that the students be there at a designated time means that you should be there at that time also. Unfortunately, some directors do not consider this important and arrive some 10 minutes or so before starting time. The players begin to get nervous, and if they have any questions or problems, there is no one with whom they can talk. Your being there gives them confidence and assurance, and they know that should an emergency arise, there is someone there who can provide immediate help.

SUGGESTIONS REGARDING
ATTIRE FOR PERFORMANCES

It has usually been customary for band players to have special uniforms. This is not always so with orchestras; however, some sort of uniform dress is quite often decided upon. This has an advantage; if a certain form of dress is chosen, no one will be conspicuous by his or her selection of apparel. Nothing should be worn that will draw attention away from the music and toward the individuals. This can be explained to the students when they are discussing what to do about dress for concerts.

The matter does have to be discussed; people always want to know what to wear for certain occasions, especially when they are going to be viewed by an audience. Some groups decide to have rather conservative, formal attire for regular concerts and more casual dress for "Pops" or other less formal affairs. Some schools purchase white coats for the boys to wear with dark trousers; however, with styles changing often, this may not be feasible and seems to be a poor investment. If the students provide their own, they can use them at other times also.

Wearing dark suits and long black dresses or dressy black pantsuits is being done a lot for formal concerts. The dresses or pantsuits should not be extreme in style, as this attracts attention to individuals. (''Loud'' socks on the boys can do the same thing.)

Sometimes girls will get ''carried away'' with a current fashion and want to have dresses alike in that style. This is fine, but I have one word of caution: dresses made of heavy material with high necks and long sleeves can be very warm, and when dressed in this way and exercising as in playing an instrument, one may become very uncomfortable. If the weather is warm and there is no air conditioning, students have been known to faint; this can even happen on a warm stage in winter. If the weather is extremely warm, the girls can be encouraged to wear something light and the boys can play without coats.

Tight-fitting clothing can restrict freedom of movement and proper breathing and impair, to some extent, the execution of the music.

These are things to be aware of in discussing the dress for concerts. Whatever is chosen should be in good taste. This will add to the stature of the orchestra and make it appear neat, refined, and cultured. (It goes without saying that everyone should also be well-groomed, which includes well-shined shoes.)

WHAT SHOULD NOT BE DONE

Sometimes we have to mention the negative in order to achieve the positive. The audience can give full attention to the music instead of critical notice to negative factors if the following ''don'ts'' are observed.

Don't:

1. Chew gum. I cannot think of one logical excuse for any player to chew gum. Of course, this applies mainly to string and percussion players; however, I have seen wind players chewing in rhythm during rests. This is a most annoying sight.

2. Tap feet. If the orchestra is well-rehearsed, no player need tap his foot. This type of display is usually evident in a jazz combo or sometimes a stage band, but has no place in the orchestra.

3. Cross legs or ankles. In addition to giving a sloppy appearance, this causes poor posture which leads to poor playing.

4. Talk during concert. Unless it is absolutely necessary, there should be no talking at all during rests in the performance of a selection. Any talking between selections should be held to a minimum, and then should only be something directly related to the performance. Anything else can wait.

5. Turn pages noisily. With some practice, pages can be turned smoothly. The surest way to be quiet is to prepare to turn the page about two or three bars before the end of the line. This will prevent

haste which usually ends in the procedure being noisy. Generally wind and percussion parts are printed so that ample time is available for turning the page.

6. Wear perfume. This may seem to be a small matter, but it can cause an allergy in some people, resulting in sneezing and coughing.

7. Wear flashy jewelry. Something simple causes no objections, but noticeably showy jewelry again causes the individual to be conspicuous. Necklaces should be avoided by violin and viola players and tie clips by cellists, as they can cause rattles.

8. Display poor posture. If the performers maintain good posture and playing positions, they are alert and ready to do their best.

9. Put music on the floor. All music should be kept on the music stand. If, by accident, a sheet falls to the floor, it should be picked up as soon as the selection in progress is finished.

Chapter 11

How to Rehearse
with Soloists and / or Chorus

Rehearsing with a soloist or chorus (or both) and an orchestra presents a variety of challenges which, unless resolved beforehand, can slow down the effectiveness of several rehearsal sessions. As with any rehearsal, a definite procedure must be planned to make adequate use of the allotted time.

Keep in mind that the average high school orchestra players have had very little experience in accompaniment. Usually they are the prime performers. Playing "second fiddle" to a soloist or chorus requires a change in attitude. The group members must understand that their part, while considered subordinate, is still very vital. They may have to subdue their playing at times, but the support has to be there or the whole performance will fall apart. If you can get your players in the correct frame of mind beforehand, you will have fewer difficulties later on.

There are five points that you should give attention to when considering whether or not to have a soloist or chorus perform with your orchestra:

1. How much time can be devoted to rehearsing with the soloist or chorus? Will the work be performed more than once? Will the values gained be worth the time spent on such rehearsals?
2. The ability of the orchestra will help determine the difficulty of accompaniment that can be done. Many compositions for soloist or chorus and orchestra are beyond the realm of the average high school

group. Be sure the orchestra can do justice to the selection or selections requested.

3. Has the soloist or the chorus performed with an orchestra before? If not, more time will be needed for rehearsing.

4. Is the soloist or chorus of high school level, professional, or semi-professional?

5. Under what kind of conditions will the performance take place? Will it be necessary to move equipment out of the school?

INSTRUMENTAL SOLOISTS

Often a high school orchestra has at least one player capable of performing a solo with the orchestra. If he is an outstanding player, the instrument he plays is secondary. A good performance on any instrument for which a work has been written will be pleasing to an audience. You should encourage the above-average player to avail himself of the opportunity of performing with the orchestra. It will also give the orchestra members the experience of accompanying a soloist.

Five Procedures to Follow

1. Obviously, a student this advanced will be studying privately. If he is interested in playing a solo with the orchestra, your first step is to talk with the private teacher if you have not already been contacted by him or her. He will know best whether or not the student is ready to attempt such an undertaking.

2. Go over the work with the student and teacher at one of the private lessons. This will give you insight into the interpretation the student is mastering.

3. Next, work with the student and the accompanist (if not a piano solo). If you conduct at this time, the soloist can get accustomed to watching the beat out of the corner of his eye. (You should also work with a piano soloist alone before doing it with the orchestra.) The tempo should be kept as strict as possible, allowing, of course, for interpretative nuances. With an orchestra playing accompaniment, rather than one person who can follow him, it will be quite different for the soloist. The whole orchestra cannot easily "catch up" if he hurries.

4. While rehearsals with the soloist are being done, rehearse the orchestra during the regular rehearsal period (without the soloist). After a few rehearsals, take time to play a recording or tape of the composition, if available. Becoming acquainted with the way in which the selection fits together is very helpful in learning the accompaniment.

5. The next step is to bring the soloist and orchestra together. At this first meeting, a general run-through is called for, with as few stops as possible. If neither the soloist nor the orchestra members have ever rehearsed under these conditions, both are in for a treat; they will hear a new sound—one they haven't heard before.

Piano Soloist

A pianist should be seated so that he can look up and see you. It is best to put the piano lid up all the way. You should stand behind the lid, thus being somewhat hidden from the audience. This will help focus attention on the soloist and not on the conductor. Also, the piano will be heard better with the lid up reflecting the sound into the audience. If the lid is removed completely, the sound will go up somewhat instead of out. Simulating these conditions as nearly as possible during rehearsals will get everyone accustomed to the way it will be at the performance.

When my high school orchestra presented a 30-minute program on a Portland, Oregon, TV station, one of the selections was a piano solo with orchestra, Grieg's *Piano Concerto in A Minor* (first movement, with cut). Because of the special camera angles the director desired, it was necessary to alter the position of the orchestra as well as that of the piano. The orchestra players were seated in the usual arrangement, but there were aisles between them to permit freedom of camera movement for different shots. The piano was to my left, but farther away than usual so as not to obscure the other players (Figure 11-1). For the same reason, the lid was removed. In this instance, of course, the sound engineer could increase the piano volume if necessary.

Other Soloists

A soloist on another instrument should stand (or sit) somewhat to your left, yet not so far out that he cannot see you out of the corner of his left eye. This does not mean that he has to be perfectly still in one spot. One year at our spring concert, we featured a student soloist playing Artie Shaw's *Concerto for Clarinet and Orchestra*. Since this was a jazz-type selection, the soloist felt that moving about a bit as he played expressed the mood better than standing still. I was in accord with this, since he was very talented and steady, and was always where he could see me whenever there was an important entrance or ritard, etc.

Values of Memorization

I have always insisted that the soloist memorize the work he is to perform. My reasoning is that when the selection is solid in the mind of the player, he can give full attention to the accompanying group as well as to his own

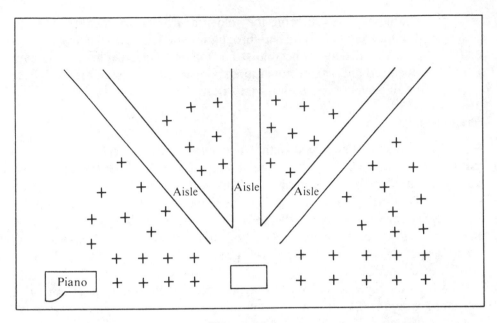

Figure 11-1

performance of the solo part. Also, there will not be the need for someone to be on stage to turn pages, nor for a music stand. (Some pianists have told me that they feel more at ease with no music staring them in the face.)

Monitor Balance between Soloist and Ensemble

Ordinarily, in a regular concert in an auditorium or gym, I feel that a sound system should not be used. My personal experience has been that a better balance is achieved without amplification unless the orchestra is also amplified and a trained sound engineer is available. This is usually not the case.

The delicate balance between playing too loudly or too softly so that the soloist can't hear the orchestra is one you have to work out carefully. At dress rehearsals I go out into the audience area to listen, at times, or ask someone else to do this so that the balance can be checked.

Tempo: An Important Concern

The soloist should be permitted, within reason, to set the tempo of the work. He best knows how fast he is able to execute the most difficult passages. On the other hand, he must be made aware of the fact that certain sections may be nearly impossible for the orchestra to play clearly at the tempo he suggests. A compromise must be worked out between you and the soloist. It is more important that the performance be clear and musical (even if it means slowing the tempo slightly) than that a metronome marking be exactly observed. Tempo is always a critical factor, particularly with students, since there is usually a tendency to rush. (This is especially true in the more difficult passages—in order to get through with them quickly, I suppose!) When this happens it can be quite difficult to return to the original tempo unless there is a fermata or a G. P.

Professional Soloist

Occasionally you might have a professional or semi-professional instrumental soloist perform with your orchestra. In this case the routine would be similar to that just mentioned, but you probably wouldn't need as many rehearsals together, since a professional would be able to maintain a more steady tempo, etc. (You would still have to rehearse the orchestra parts as much.) Of course, in the case of the professional, you would not be conferring with an instructor ahead of time, only with the person himself.

VOCAL SOLOISTS

When rehearsing with vocal soloists, some of the same procedures used in working with instrumentalists apply. You should discuss the songs selected with the private vocal coach (except in the case of a professional) and rehearse with the soloist and accompanist before doing it with the orchestra. Again, playing a recording or tape will be of help while the orchestra parts are being learned. Also, balance should be checked carefully, as with instrumental soloists. In the case of a professional vocalist, the comments concerning professional instrumental soloists would apply.

Basic Differences between Vocal and Instrumental Soloists

In rehearsing with vocal soloists, the following points should be kept in mind:

1. Except in the case of a professional, the voice probably is not mature enough to project over an orchestra of 50 or more players. (There are exceptions. I've heard a few high school vocalists who could hold their own with a full-sized orchestra, but this is not usually the case.) Under most circumstances it is best to cut the size of the orchestra down, yet keep an adequate balance. Usually the instrumentation is not overly heavy for a vocal solo accompaniment, and you may need to cut down only on the number of string players. How you do this is up to you. I usually use the first violins and the principal and perhaps assistant principal of the seconds. They can be divided into two sections for first and second violin parts. For the other parts I use the best players, usually those sitting on the outside in each section.

Many times one string bass player is all that is required. The players not needed can be excused early to study or practice while you rehearse the accompaniment.

2. The first rehearsal or two can present a problem for a singer, unless he or she has sung with an orchestra before. Up until this time the soloist has been rehearsing with piano, which is really a percussive instrument. The inexperienced soloist may find that during the first few times with the orchestra, it may seem as if the bottom has dropped out of the accompaniment. This is due to the more legato effect of the orchestra as compared with the piano. The piano tends to play each beat a bit louder because of the hammer action. There may be a slight lapse in the sense of pitch by the singer, but this will soon be overcome as the rehearsals progress and confidence is gained. At each rehearsal the soloist should stand approximately where he will stand at the performance; this will help him become accustomed to the sound of the orchestra and to watching you.

3. Phrasing should be given special attention because allowance must be made for the singer to take breaths. Breath marks should be in your score and on all parts involved. Sometimes the orchestra holds on when the soloist stops to breathe; in that case, only your score need be marked as a reminder to prolong the beat after the soloist stops.

4. It should be remembered that rehearsals should not be as long as with instrumental soloists. (Usually vocal solos are not as lengthy as instrumental anyway). Little can be accomplished if the singer's voice gives out.

CHORUS

Many of the same considerations that are necessary when rehearsing with soloists also apply when a chorus is involved. The same pre-orchestral procedures should be followed as with soloists. The rehearsals and performances will, in many cases, be conducted by the orchestral director. Therefore, you should be somewhat acquainted with the details of vocal music; it also helps to have had some training and experience in directing a combination such as this (during college or in working with a seasoned director).

My first experience in directing a combined choir and orchestra came when I was a sophomore in college. It is one I'll never forget. To help with my expenses, I had secured a position as a church choir director. It was customary for that church to present special music on Easter Sunday and, undaunted, I agreed to have something "special." I chose *Unfold, Ye Portals* by Gounod as the selection, and invited singers from the college choir to participate in order to augment the church choir. Since I also played in the college orchestra, I asked the members of this group if they would play for this special program. It was not a very large orchestra and so I used it in its entirety. I rehearsed each group individually, and the Thursday evening before Easter had one combined rehearsal which went very well. On Sunday, it was somewhat of a different story.

Since the instrumentation was quite complete, I would have preferred to perform without the organ; however, the elderly lady who played the organ was very faithful and quite competent, and so I included her. She was situated on my left on the floor; the orchestra was on an improvised stage. In order for her to see me, she used a mirror. As we prepared to perform, I looked at her and she nodded, indicating that she was ready. The selection began smoothly. About one-third of the way along, I began to notice a polyphonic effect and realized that the organ was a full measure ahead of the choir and orchestra. Frantically I looked at the organist and made a gesture, but she just smiled at me.

While this "unwritten" polyphonic style continued, my mind groped for a solution to the predicament; I realized that this could not go on until the end. What could be done? Since it seemed impossible to get the organist back with the rest of us, the only thing left to do was to bring the choir and orchestra up to where she was. The only opportunity for this would be during one measure of interlude by the orchestra before the recapitulation.

The choir and orchestra members were aware that something was amiss. (I could see it in the way they looked at me.) This was good, since it meant that I would have their undivided attention. I decided to do the "catching up" during that measure rest for the choir simply by not giving them that measure, but indicating the pickup beat for their next entrance instead (and trying to signify to the orchestra that they should skip that bar also).

As we approached the spot, I held my left hand up for attention and cued in the choir, mouthing their word. My beat was different, of course, from what it would have been for the measure for orchestra alone, and most of the players caught it right away. There were a couple of ragged beats, but we got back together and from then on all was well.

I didn't have the heart to say anything to the organist. She told me after the service that the loose section in the middle of her music had fallen to the floor and she couldn't stop playing to pick it up, so she played that whole section from memory! I don't know whether or not she ever realized that anything was wrong. I'm really sorry that we didn't have tape recorders in those days—I've always wondered just how that sounded. I was too occupied to listen with any degree of objectivity.

This experience taught me just how alert a conductor must be at every moment. It's somewhat akin to driving a car in traffic—we never know just what type of situation may develop. In the many years since that incident, several little unforeseen difficulties have arisen and I have had to plan quickly for an "escape route." Sometimes an unusual gesture will call attention to the problem and it is corrected; at times I have had to cut short a wrong or out-of-tune note or chord. Conversely, when something is particularly beautiful, I prolong it just a bit, but not so long that it loses the effect. We do have to do some on-the-spot quick thinking at times!

Seven Very Important Concerns

You should keep in mind the following seven important points in order to insure profitable rehearsals with chorus and orchestra:

1. You are dealing with not one singer, but many. The number can vary from 20 to 100 or more.
2. The size of the group and its maturity and tonal power will determine how large an orchestra to use. The selection(s) will also help decide this.
3. The choral group may be directed and trained by another director.
4. It will be necessary for the chorus to become adjusted to a rather different style of conducting from that which the regular director employs. While orchestral conducting consists of a rather precise beat (especially for student orchestras), choral directors often find it possible to conduct more freely, even to specific notes or words.
5. The chorus, unlike a soloist, cannot be standing in front of the orchestra; therefore, a different arrangement must be used.
6. When conducting a chorus and orchestra together, there is likely to be more of a beat lag than with either one alone, because of the distance involved when the chorus is behind the orchestra or is on stage with the orchestra in the pit.
7. Rehearsal time may be a problem, since most likely the orchestra and chorus do not meet during the same period. Arrangements may have to be made for chorus members to be excused from class to come to rehearsal during orchestra period. If only a small orchestra is required, it might be more suitable to do the opposite. As few rehearsals together as possible will promote a good rapport with other school departments. A rehearsal or two might have to be scheduled before or after school (or in the evening).

Steps to Take

If you are the choral as well as the orchestral director, some of the following will not apply but will be done automatically:

1. Sit in on several rehearsals with the chorus (after going over the work with the choral director), and observe what is being done. This will enable you to become acquainted with the interpretation toward

which the group is working. (Whatever the interpretation, it is his privilege since it is his group.) Also, you will become aware of any conducting problems you may have to solve when the two groups get together. If it is not possible for you to be free very often at the time the chorus rehearses, you will need extra conferences with the director. Arrangements can usually be made to free you for a limited number of such visits.

2. The next step is for you to "take over" the chorus for a couple of rehearsals, if possible. (If #1 is not possible, this, at least, should be done so that the chorus members will become a little familiar with your conducting before meeting with the orchestra.) This can save considerable time and confusion; at least some things can be worked out during your "guest" appearances.

3. While steps 1 and 2 are being executed, the orchestra will be rehearsing its parts that have been marked as to bowing, phrasing, letters or numbers, repeats, breath marks, etc.

4. Arrangements are then made for placing the chorus. As a rule, it is most convenient for the rehearsal to take place in the orchestral room. It is easier to move a chorus and risers than music stands, chairs, and percussion instruments (unless just a small orchestra is required). In most cases the chorus is placed behind the orchestra and on risers. The latter is necessary for two reasons: the singers are able to see you, and can be heard better over the orchestra than if on the flat floor. If the chorus is a chamber choir of around 20 singers, I place them to one side of the orchestra, usually on my left at somewhat of an angle as in Figure 11-2. A small number of singers can be heard more easily

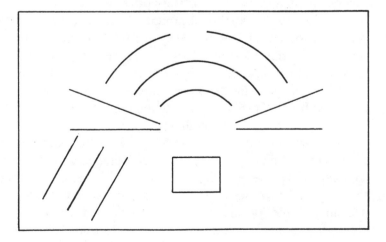

Figure 11-2

if placed in this manner rather than behind the orchestra. If a chamber orchestra is used, it is possible to place the chorus members on both sides of the conductor, in front and at an angle to the orchestra. A small orchestra of 12-18 strings, woodwinds, and a few brass can be positioned as in Figure 11-3. The size and depth of the stage may

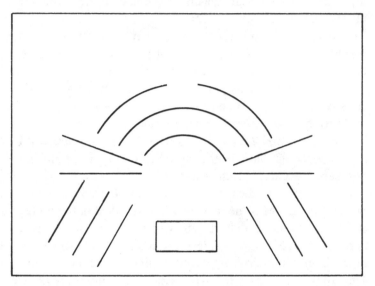

Figure 11-3

dictate, to some extent, how the chorus is situated at the performance. An arrangement similar to one of those in Figure 11-2 or Figure 11-3 can be worked out with small groups, and is a change from the usual "chorus behind the orchestra" set-up.

5. When directing the combined group, you must increase the size of your beat somewhat, yet still keep it in relationship to the volume desired. Attention must also be given to the height of the beat. The tendency is to raise the arms higher than is necessary for the chorus to see. If they're too high, the orchestra players, particularly those close to you, will have difficulty in watching both the beat and the music (especially if you are on a podium).

6. The dynamics of the chorus should be increased when singing with an orchestra, and the singers must be encouraged to maintain this and not weaken as the rehearsal progresses. Of course, the orchestra must be subdued, sometimes to just a whisper in extremely soft passages.

7. If at all possible (depending on the length of the choral work), the vocal parts should be memorized. This will insure 100% attention to the conductor who is considerably farther away from them than usual.

There are, of course, choral works that, by tradition, are not memorized, e.g., Handel's *Messiah*, a *Mass* or *Requiem*, etc.

8. When rehearsing a full period with a chorus and orchestra, it is best to have a break every 15 minutes or so for the chorus members to sit for a moment on the risers or at least to stretch and move just a bit. To stand motionless for 50 minutes or more and sing can be very tiring and cause poor attention and restlessness. (If the performance is long there should be a couple of intermissions.) Special attention must be given to the ventilation in the rehearsal room and stage area, because there will probably be twice the usual number of people in the room. Also, if the orchestra is on built-in risers, the chorus being on risers will put some of the singers close to the ceiling where the heat concentrates. During such rehearsals I lower the room temperature a bit and check to be sure there is enough circulation of air.

9. At least one rehearsal should take place where the performance is to be held. If it is in the school auditorium or gym, the only things to be done are to move the equipment for the orchestra and the risers for the chorus. If it is to be any distance from the school, a truck will have to be used and several students enlisted to help in the moving to and from the site.

    If the auditorium has a fairly large pit, the orchestra can be there. The chorus will then be at the front of the stage and will have the advantage of being heard with somewhat less strain. The gym might be used for a performance by a large chorus and orchestra. A good arrangement for this is to have the chorus behind the orchestra and a wall behind the chorus. A choral shell also helps in projecting the singing toward the audience (Figure 11-4). If only one side of the bleachers is to be used for the audience, I prefer to rearrange the set-up as in Figure 11-5. Here no one in the audience need sit at an angle in order to have visual contact with the performers. Usually there is time for only one dress rehearsal at the performance site, and, if in a gym, you must keep in mind that more volume is needed than in an auditorium. The chorus should be encouraged to sing out at this rehearsal, even though it seems exceptionally loud. They should not, of course, sacrifice tone for volume. When the room is filled with people, a portion of the volume will be absorbed, and the final presentation should be correct as far as volume is concerned.

Non-School Chorus

If the chorus is one from the community (rather than the school choir), the same procedure should take place, except that the rehearsals will probably have

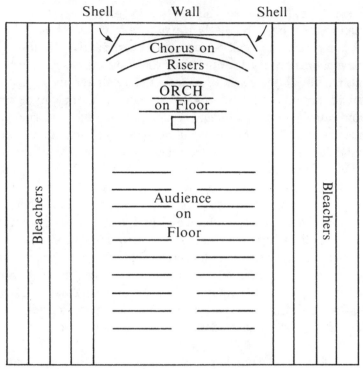

Figure 11-4

Figure 11-5

to be held in the evening. Since this would probably be a chorus of adults, most of them would not be available during the day. If the orchestra is well-prepared and you rehearse with the chorus several times beforehand so that they become accustomed to your directing, probably one or two rehearsals together will be enough. One should definitely be held at the performance site in order to check out the balance and the physical arrangements of seating and standing.

Sometimes two or more school or community choirs may be combined to sing a work with orchestral accompaniment. In this case, probably one dress rehearsal will be all that can be arranged. You should work with each chorus alone and have them together at least once before the dress rehearsal. In the event that one of the choir directors is to conduct the performance, he must also work with the orchestra alone a time or two before putting it all together.

CHORUS AND SOLOISTS WITH ORCHESTRA

It is possible that for some occasion you might wish to perform a work that includes soloists and chorus with the orchestra. The same rehearsal procedures mentioned before also apply in this situation: work with the chorus alone and soloists alone, then with the orchestra.

Definite Schedule Important

When the time comes to work together, you should have a time schedule made out, since there are so many people involved. Giving out instructional sheets can be of help; everyone should have the time and place of rehearsal in writing. Each person must understand that it is important that he be where he is supposed to be at the proper time so that no one else's time will be wasted in waiting.

The work may contain numbers with solo and orchestra alone, as well as some for chorus and orchestra alone. If the rehearsals are held during school time, probably everyone will have to be present during the entire period. Sometimes it might be possible to have the choral numbers first and excuse these people while you work on the solos; if not, they will have to sit quietly and listen while the soloists rehearse.

If the rehearsals are not during school hours, the choral numbers can be first and the soloists later so that noise made by arriving chorus members can be avoided. The order might have to be reversed to accommodate a soloist, especially if he or she is not a member of the chorus.

If there are sections of the work containing chorus and soloists in one number, then, of course, these will have to be rehearsed together. They can be taken out of order, if necessary, and the soloists excused when finished. The point is that there should be a minimum of waiting to rehearse on the part of anyone.

Chapter 12

The Rehearsing
of a Musical Show

Presenting a musical show is a large undertaking. It can be very rewarding or extremely taxing and nerve-racking. Before directing such a show, you should have some experience in directing orchestra and chorus and/or soloists together.

Timing is extremely important in shows, and you have to know most of the dialogue as well as the music. Sometimes there is music under dialogue and you have to make split-second decisions as to whether or not to repeat a vamp before the singing starts.

In doing a show, you will work with the drama coach as well as with the choral director. If you are also the choral director, you will be training the chorus and soloists in addition to the orchestra.

Often there is a student assistant to the drama director, but the music is usually too difficult for a student to assist with the orchestra. You will need the best students to play anyway, and it will be enough for them to learn their parts. A teacher aide or adult assistant can be of help, however, if there is someone available. Working out difficult passages in sectionals and/or small groups will be very useful. You will need assistance with such things as publicity, tickets, ushers, programs, etc., and students can take care of these details with some supervision.

This chapter will discuss topics such as how to choose a show, when to begin rehearsals, when and how to rehearse with orchestra alone and with chorus, soloists, and dancers. Also covered are the dress rehearsals and some types of problems that could occur.

HOW TO CHOOSE A SHOW

Before any rehearsing can take place, a suitable show must be selected. The problem arises as to how this is done. It must be given careful consideration, since once a contract has been signed, changes cannot be made. We have employed the following techniques for selecting shows:

1. Observation of different musicals as presented by other schools or community or traveling groups. If a school production, we took into consideration the size of the student body, the musical and acting talents of the students, and the facilities in which the show was presented.
2. Discussion between the drama and music directors regarding past experiences in putting on such shows. Which ones were easier than others? Which types had good audience appeal? If you have never worked on a show, talking with someone who has can be of help.
3. Obtaining a published list of shows available and their range of difficulty. Also listed is the instrumentation required, which is helpful in making up the orchestra.
4. Assessing the ability of the talent with which you would work. It is easy to go beyond the capabilities of the students, which can result in a rather inferior production. The music for some shows is quite difficult for the orchestra.

REHEARSING THE ORCHESTRAL PARTS ALONE

The timetable for rehearsing the orchestral portion of a show needs to be considered carefully. Having well-planned rehearsals, utilizing every moment of the time, is essential in order to avoid as many last-minute problems as possible.

Usually the music is on a rental basis for a period of two or three months. As soon as it arrives, you must check the parts against your piano-vocal score (there is not always a full score available). This is very important because many times there are errors; sometimes we have found errors even at the first rehearsal that I didn't catch because of not having a full score. This checking is a task for you, not a student, since you will decide on any cuts or cross-cues that may be necessary. Such things should be marked in each part prior to the first rehearsal (in pencil so that they can be erased; otherwise you will be fined).

When to Start

The question of when to begin rehearsals depends largely on the difficulty of the music. My own personal preference is to start as late as possible and still have ample rehearsal time. The trick is to plan the time so that the players know that there is absolutely no time to waste in order to be ready for dress rehearsals. My experience has been that the students learn the music much faster when they realize that the deadline is not far off. If you begin too soon, the enthusiasm can wane and the spark will diminish by the time you get to dress rehearsals. If the show is to be presented during the winter months, I usually plan a little more time, since illness is more prevalent than at other times and there is the possibility of the school closing for a few days due to inclement weather.

If you use the full orchestra and can rehearse every day, you will not need as much time as if you are using a smaller group and need to rehearse at a time other than the regular orchestra period. In the latter case the sessions would probably not be daily.

Depending on the foregoing points, starting rehearsals four to six weeks before dress rehearsals would be about right.

Individual Practice Ahead of Time Can Be Effective

As soon as the parts are checked over, I give them out to the players with definite instructions to practice carefully, watching the many key changes, tricky rhythms, and repeat signs for which musical shows are noted. In short, I ask that they become well-acquainted with the music. The fact that most show music is manuscript rather than printed is an obstacle, since most students have had little experience in reading this type of music. To wait until the first run-through to hand out the parts is to invite delay; most of the time during the first rehearsal would be spent in trying to figure out the notes. Having some private practice in advance helps the players feel more sure of themselves at first rehearsal. Also, it is possible to begin the rehearsals a bit later than if they hadn't seen the music beforehand.

Scheduling Orchestral Rehearsals

If you feel that you can use the complete group, then, of course, you will use the regular orchestra period for rehearsals. Probably you will need most of the wind and percussion players (unless there is no part for an instrument), but you may not want to use all the string players since this might overpower the singers. If you have enough string people who are qualified to handle show music, you can rehearse all of them and then use alternate players at different performances. Not only does this give more students the opportunity to take part, but it allows coverage in case of illness or other emergency. If you do this, each "orchestra" should rehearse at alternate dress rehearsals so that the balance can be checked.

If you ordinarily have the winds only once or twice a week, you will probably have to arrange for some sectionals with these players unless the band director can spare them more often during this time.

You will probably have to schedule rehearsals outside of school time if you feel that you cannot use all the players in one way or another, or if the space for the orchestra in the auditorium is small, or the music is not scored for full orchestra. If it is not possible to rehearse this smaller group at another time (because of bus schedules or conflicts), the only alternative is to rehearse during the regular orchestra period and excuse the players not needed. These people might study, practice individually or in small groups, or work on other projects. You might possibly be working on some other music at the same time, and the full orchestra could rehearse on that part of the time; usually, however, the show music takes up most of the time.

How to Rehearse the Orchestra Alone

The procedure for rehearsing is very important. Here are three steps to follow for productive show rehearsals:

1. Rehearse strings alone first, if at all possible. As with any orchestral work, they usually have the most to do and many of the difficult parts. Getting these at least partly cleared up ahead of time will pay dividends later.

2. Rehearse with full orchestra, reading through the entire score before beginning to work out the fine points. Stop only when everything breaks down because of rhythmic difficulties or a series of incorrect notes. This reading-through process helps the players become acquainted with the continuity of the musical; they will discover a bit about how the whole thing fits together. Obviously, when taking a full run-through, some of the winds will have "rest periods" because their parts are tacet or nearly so. The point has been made throughout this book that the players in a section should not be idle for any length of time. However, this is the one exception. It will have to be explained to these people that, due to the nature of this type of undertaking, they will have to wait patiently for their entrances. If they know that you expect them to be mature enough to do this quietly, you will usually have no problems. From listening and watching, they will get an idea of the whole show and just when they will be playing. Also, they can benefit from directions you give the others, since they may have similar passages in other places in the music.

3. At subsequent rehearsals, work out the tough parts. If you are rehearsing during the regular orchestra period, you can take the numbers in sequence again, stopping to work on the difficult passages. If you are rehearsing at a different time, taking the selections that include all of the players first is a good idea. As they are no longer needed, they can be excused. If it is necessary for them to remain for reasons of transportation, they must understand that they should use the time for study, reading, or listening, but not talking, unless there is another area where they can wait. This procedure may eventually end with the strings alone again, which gives you an opportunity to work over a spot or two that can use the extra practice.

As these rehearsals progress, keep asking the players to play more softly on the passages for soloists. If the dynamics are not marked, insist that they put markings in the music and not rely on memory. Work toward clean playing, even though soft. It will take them a while to adjust to the idea of playing ''under'' the singers, so to speak. To wait until rehearsals with soloists and chorus is inviting unnecessary difficulties.

REHEARSING SOLOISTS, CHORUS, AND DANCERS WITH ORCHESTRA

Before having rehearsals with the soloists and chorus, you should go over the vocal numbers with them in association with the vocal coach. If you are also the choral director, you will have been rehearsing these people, naturally.

When you think the vocalists and orchestra are sufficiently prepared, arrangements should be made for rehearsing together. Doing this several times before dress rehearsals will make your work easier then. Even if you have to schedule a couple of these rehearsals after school, it will pay off.

Vocal Soloists: Encourage Flexibility

The soloists in a musical are also actors and have lines to say. I make it a practice to ask them to say several lines in order to gauge the timing necessary for the introduction (if there is one) so that they can start the song at the right moment. This will avoid awkward delays at dress rehearsals, and train the soloists in the speed of saying lines to the background of the introduction. The orchestra must be kept under the dialogue at all times, yet the singers must hear the pitch.

A soloist can take liberties such as a rubato now and then, and this should be encouraged since it makes the music more interesting than just straight rhythm. However, judgment must be exercised and this type of thing not carried to excess.

If there is motion involved and space in the rehearsal room, allow the singer to act out the part. Being in motion while singing is a valuable experience; it will accustom the soloist to hearing the orchestra from different areas of the room. When dress rehearsals begin in the auditorium, the orchestra will be in the pit, creating a new acoustical problem for the singer. Here it may sound softer and there will be a need to pay closer attention to pitch. Having had some practice in singing while in motion, the movements will be somewhat automatic, freeing the mind for careful attention to the correct pitch. There may not be much motion during a song, but usually there is at least a little.

The singer should be encouraged to "sing out" over the orchestra, and even on soft passages the orchestra must keep "under" the singer.

Any such pre-dress rehearsal practice that is feasible should be done. I am a firm believer in doing as much as possible prior to the dress rehearsals to help keep things from piling up then, causing tensions.

The Chorus Requires a New Approach

When bringing in the chorus, there is one major point you must keep in mind. The chorus members will not, in most cases, be lined up in rows nor on risers as in a concert. Instead, they will be scattered, yet close enough to hear one another. In some shows they walk around and across the stage while singing.

At the first rehearsals with the orchestra I keep the chorus close together, usually in front and to one side of the orchestra. It is necessary that the chorus and orchestra "fit like a glove" before freedom of movement is allowed. After things go well together, you can have the singers in the chorus stand approximately in the positions that blocking has taught them and go through some of their motions as they sing (if space permits).

Combining Chorus and Soloists with Orchestra

The next step is to rehearse the selections involving both chorus and soloists. If there is not enough space for them to move about, they can be arranged as in Figure 12-1.

At this point special attention should be given to balance. While this is not the site of the performance (and when on stage, balance will be checked many times) being alert to how the numbers go together in this respect is very important.

Rehearsing with Dancers: Rhythmical Precision Necessary

It is a good idea to arrange a rehearsal or two with the dancers before dress rehearsals. If there isn't enough space in the rehearsal room, another site will have to be found and the orchestra moved. It can be done in the auditorium or

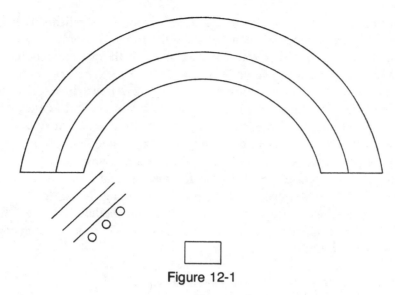

Figure 12-1

the gym or some multipurpose room in the school. First choice, of course, is where the performances will take place. If any other place is used, the area needed by the dancers should be marked off so that it will be exactly the same as the stage. Masking tape is satisfactory for this.

If the choreography is being done by someone within the school, probably a rehearsal can be arranged sometime during the school day or immediately after school. If a choreographer has been brought in from the outside, perhaps an evening rehearsal or two will have to be held.

If you can make a tape of the dance music early in your rehearsals, this is helpful to the dancers. If the music is too difficult to do this effectively soon enough for them to rehearse with, they can use piano or a tape of the piano part. In either case it is a good idea for them to rehearse with piano the first few times because of the percussive effect; they will get accustomed to the beat easier than if they work with an orchestra tape right away. However, you should instruct the orchestra players from the beginning to emphasize the strong beats and to play out for the dancing (unless they have to subdue slightly because of dialogue or singing). In any event, it will probably take a little time for the dancers to adjust to the orchestra. Eventually the attacks may be softened somewhat, but never should they become weak or indistinct. There must be a constant flow of precise rhythm since it is impossible for the dancers to watch you while dancing.

ARRANGE AN ALL-MUSICAL REHEARSAL

If time permits, it is an excellent idea to have one evening or late afternoon rehearsal at the performance site for all the musical portions of the show.

It should be held sometime within the week before dress rehearsals begin so that any obvious weaknesses can be worked on before going into the final rehearsals. Also, at this time you can talk to all of the participants regarding points that may pertain to everyone.

This rehearsal can be accomplished in a 2-2½ hour time period with a 15-minute break. No high school group can maintain peak efficiency for that long without a little rest. True, performances are strenuous, but students get a break between acts and during the dialogue. The people acting get some rest also since they are not all on stage during the entire show.

I begin this rehearsal promptly at the time set, and everyone knows this. Punctuality must be observed or people will be coming in for 15-20 minutes after they should have been there. A definite time schedule must be followed throughout the rehearsal. It's easy to forget how fast the time is going and stay on one number too long.

Distribute Instructional Notices Ahead of Time

At least three weeks before this rehearsal is to take place, an instructional sheet with time schedules for it and the dress rehearsals should be given out so that everyone can plan to be present. These can be passed out even earlier if the date for the mass rehearsal is set.

Also on this sheet can be performance information, including when to arrive, where to meet, and what to wear. (The performance dates should have been known by everyone since being set.) If all these facts are in writing, no one can say he didn't know what time to be there, etc.

Rehearse Chorus and Orchestra First

I start with the choral and orchestral numbers because if the orchestra rehearses alone or with soloists first, the chorus members will begin arriving and invariably start to talk—softly at first, but gradually the volume will increase. Even adult choir members are not always quiet when they arrive at a rehearsal of this type. It's a human trait for people to talk when they get together, so why fight it? If you start with the chorus, you'll avoid having to stop to ask them to be quiet.

The chorus members should practice wherever they will be located for their numbers and go through any motions they are to do.

Numbers with Chorus, Soloists, and Orchestra Next

Usually selections for soloists and chorus together are fewer in number than those involving chorus or soloists alone. Therefore, this portion of the rehearsal will probably take less time. Any action in conjunction with the singing should be practiced here also.

When the desired results are achieved (or the time limit has been reached), dismiss the chorus. This is a good time for the orchestra members to "take five" while the chorus people are leaving.

Soloists and Orchestra

Now go over the solos, again including any necessary motions. There should be no confusion, since the chorus members are finished and excused.

Rehearse Orchestral Selections Alone

This is optional. If you have plenty of rehearsal time left, you may want to stop at this point. If you feel you need this time for rehearsal, you might want to go over any rough spots that need touching up. In the effort to get the accompaniments "down pat," the special orchestral selections such as the overture, entr'acte, dance music, and exit music may be somewhat overlooked, and you may wish to do some work on these at this time. Unless done well, they can mar an otherwise fine performance.

Where Do the Dancers Fit In?

Up until now nothing has been said about working with the dancers at this comprehensive musical rehearsal. You may have to rehearse with them at a separate time, depending on circumstances. If you have them at this time, the musical itself dictates when. If the singing and dancing are interwoven and the dancers are also in the chorus, they can practice at the time the chorus does. If there are solo dances or groups of people who do nothing but dance, they can go through their routines when everyone except the orchestra has been excused. In this case you might wish to dispense with rehearsing any orchestral parts alone. You will be aware of when the dancers will rehearse in advance, and can regulate the time as you see fit.

THE DRESS REHEARSALS

Once the entire cast has arrived at the point of dress rehearsals, it will become obvious just how well the previous rehearsals have accomplished their purposes. All of the detailed work should have been done by now; the dress rehearsals are merely for putting the final touches on the production, seeing how make-up and costumes look under the lights, and checking the balance of sound, the P.A. system (if one is used), and the timing.

Since there are usually two or more such rehearsals, it is possible to plan several constructive steps to insure a top-notch performance.

The First Dress Rehearsal

My preference at the first dress rehearsal is to have the orchestra ready to start 20 minutes or so before beginning the actual show. This time is used to go over any selections or portions thereof needing attention.

As a rule, something goes wrong on this occasion to delay the start —someone is late getting make-up on, some lights are not working, a prop is missing—the list is endless. I speak from experience. This usually gives you some additional time to work with the orchestra or even a soloist or two if they are ready and waiting. In the latter case the curtain should be closed to eliminate as much backstage noise as possible. Sometimes this time can be used to talk with the orchestra and/or soloists concerning certain spots to watch carefully. *I never allow time to be wasted.*

Once the rehearsal gets under way, it should be done as it will be at the performance. The overture should be played, the house lights dimmed, and everyone is onstage or in the wings, and quiet. The actors must get accustomed to being quiet backstage. All these things will get everyone in the mood of the show. Some people will probably be in the audience, especially the drama and choral directors who should see the rehearsal under actual performance conditions.

During this rehearsal I don't stop the whole show for minor problems (they can be talked over at intermission or after rehearsal). The idea is to go through the entire performance to get the continuity. All blocking will have been worked out on the stage previous to this time, so that should not present a problem. Sometimes, because of acoustics, a few changes have to be made in the dynamics of the music.

At this rehearsal I allow the orchestra members to watch the stage action, and inform them that two quiet taps on my stand with the baton will be their signal to get in position to play.

Usually the drama director talks to all the cast after the rehearsal to point out places to improve. The orchestra members should be instructed to leave quietly so as not to disturb this discussion.

What to Do at Subsequent Dress Rehearsals

Now comes the time for each detail to be perfected as far as possible. This includes portions that were out of balance or off in timing, late entrances, poor intonation, etc. Also, the orchestra players should watch such things as turning pages noisily, plucking strings, talking during dialogue, or anything else that would detract from the show. They can be instructed to turn off their stand lights during extended stage action so that the audience will have an uninterrupted view of the stage.

Also, no taps of the baton will now be given for attention. The only indication will be that the baton is slightly raised (if raised too high, the vision of the audience can be obstructed). Time for getting into position to play should be shortened, since too long in this position before a song begins detracts from the performance.

I make it a point now and then to go out into the audience area (both downstairs and balcony) to determine the balance. By now the orchestra should be able to play a few lines without the conductor; however, I usually do this during a part in which there are no tempo changes or ritards in prospect for a while. One of the most crucial elements to watch is that of the orchestra playing too loud. If pre-dress rehearsal techniques on playing under the singing have been stressed, this problem should be somewhat less of a hassle.

I insist that the entire show should be rehearsed, as they say, "from the top" at dress rehearsals. Some directors take the show out of sequence, but I feel that continuity is necessary to master all parts—dialogue and music. Also, each person in the show must "rehearse" what he is to do when *not* on stage. Unless the show is done in sequence, this will become a problem on performance nights.

Show Should Be Timed

At the last dress rehearsal the show should be timed. The approximate time that it will be over can be determined and this information released when called for by parents or patrons. Also, the length of the intermission can be ascertained by what has to be done during that time.

A Preview Audience Can Be of Value

We usually have had at least two dress rehearsals plus a preview for students, teachers, and others (such as senior citizens) either without admission or at a reduced price. This can be done for two reasons: 1) to allow more seating for patrons at the performances, and 2) to give the cast an "audience" to help overcome nervousness on opening night.

If possible, this preview should be held the night before the first public performance. If there is no such preview, the last dress rehearsal should be then. To permit several days to elapse between the last rehearsal and first performance may cause much loss in continuity and perfection.

WHAT YOU CAN DO IF SOMEONE
ELSE CONDUCTS THE PERFORMANCES

So far in this discussion it has been assumed that you, the orchestra director, would be conducting the show in performances. However, sometimes the choral director is the one who does it, or each of you may conduct at alternate times, that is, alternate years; it is best not to change conductors during a run of the same show.

If you are not to direct the performances, you will still be training the orchestra and the procedures outlined would apply. Instead of your working with the chorus and soloists so that they can become accustomed to your directing, the choral director will have to visit the orchestra a few times for the same reason.

You can work together on the musical details of the show. Also, you can assist at the mass musical rehearsal and dress rehearsals by listening for balance and helping out with any problems that might arise in the orchestra.

EXPECT SOME EMERGENCIES TO ARISE

Many problems can occur in planning, rehearsing, or performing a show, and you have to use your best judgment in solving them (sometimes it has to be a fast decision). Problems are not usually the same in any two cases; however, following are three experiences of mine that I considered major problems. Being aware of these might help in thinking things out ahead of time.

On one occasion when I directed a show, arrangements were not made soon enough and the auditorium was already booked. The dates were set and rehearsals were in progress, and so we had to find another site. We used the gym (which had a stage), but it was a rather poor substitute and a lot of adjusting had to be done because of acoustics. Whoever is in charge of making the arrangements should take care of this sort of thing as soon as it is decided to have a show. You, as the conductor, can't do everything yourself, but this is one thing you should check on to be sure that it is done.

Often things can be overlooked during the rehearsals because all of the concentration is on the performers and not on audience reaction. At one of the shows I directed there was a duet that had two verses with a short interlude between. On opening night the audience burst into very loud applause following the first verse. I went on with the interlude, hoping that the singers could maintain the pitch. They did falter a bit on their entrance.

The next night, just before going on, the singers came to me and asked if I would change my original plan to play the interlude even louder to making a G.P. until the applause died down. This was agreeable to me; however, the problem was that the orchestra members were already in the pit, making it difficult to communicate with them. Knowing that my players had been trained to watch the baton at all times, I felt confident that I could execute the G.P. and have all of them observe it. When we approached the spot, I raised my left hand for attention and at the proper moment gave a cutoff and the entire group stopped. I don't say that this would work 100% of the time, but when a group is well-prepared and trained to be alert, such unexpected incidents can usually be handled successfully. (I always make it a point to play a few tricks in rehearsals such as holding out a beat, speeding up, or cutting off at an unexpected place in the music just in case some unforeseen situation arises during a performance.)

Another emergency problem arose during the presentation of a different show. In this case the performance was at a local theater, being part of the celebration of the 50th Anniversary of the founding of the City of Longview, Washington. In the cast and orchestra were high school, college, and community people.

This theater had not been used for a stage play for many years, and we had some electrical problems at rehearsals. However, we thought everything was working well by performance time. On opening night (again) during interlude music between scenes, the curtain rose about two feet and stopped. The music had been timed to coincide with the movement on stage and the entrance of the chorus. I began to slow the tempo somewhat to gain time, knowing that I must bring it back up before the chorus started singing or it would drag. There was a bit of noise backstage as they tried to solve the problem, and so I brought up the volume and tempo of the music, hoping that the singers would hear well enough to make the entrance since they couldn't see me for a cue. This was what actually happened. The singers were able to sing without much noticeable difficulty. Just after they began the song, the curtain cooperated and was raised. I suppose if it had stalled much longer we would have had to stop and wait for the difficulty to be corrected and then start back before the entrance of the chorus. I know that the audience would have understood that there was nothing we could do about the technical difficulty. Since it turned out that we could go on and didn't have to stop, I was glad that the orchestra members were trained to be watchful at all times so we could stay together.

This sort of problem can't be anticipated, of course, but making good use of all available rehearsal time to train the orchestra and cast members to know their parts well and to be very alert will sometimes get you out of a "tight spot."

Chapter 13

Model Rehearsal Guides
for Two Orchestral Works

In this chapter, specific ways of rehearsing two separate orchestral works will be discussed. The selections chosen represent two different periods in musical development: baroque and 20th Century. The various rehearsal techniques described in the previous chapters may be applied here.

For the director who is primarily a wind person, some bowings and fingerings have been indicated in the examples given. While there may be different ways to bow or finger a passage, the ones used here have been chosen for the best results with average high school players. Wherever possible, bowings have been kept as professional players might perform them.

It is unfortunate that orchestra players are not able to have before them the entire score (as is the case in a chorus). Since this is not possible, there are four things that can be done to aid in developing the understanding of the work:

1. Hold up the full score and point out similarities between parts, etc.
2. Show slides of the score. These can be made by photographing portions or all of the score with a 35 mm. camera. (This should be done only on selections that are in the public domain.)
3. Use an overhead projector to show the score.
4. Make miniature scores available to any player interested in following them while listening to recordings. Some libraries have these, or you can lend personal copies if you have them. One of my former vio-

linists (concertmaster), who is now a symphony conductor, began his
score reading in this manner.

PRELUDE AND FUGUE IN D MINOR
Handel – Arr. Kindler*

This baroque selection was chosen for three specific reasons: 1) it is easy
enough for the average high school orchestra to do well; 2) it contains the
essentials of baroque style; 3) it is an example of a worthwhile arrangement.
The last fact permits the entire orchestra to participate rather than the reduced
number of instruments so common to the baroque.

In looking over the score, we find that in the woodwind section there are
the usual instruments and also parts for piccolo, bass clarinet, and English
horn. There are four horn parts, a third trumpet, three trombones, and tuba.
Players of these instruments never get to perform baroque music in its original
form, and this is an advantage here. Of course, you may not have some of these
instruments, but you will have trombones, tuba, probably a piccolo, and you
may be able to get four horn and three trumpet players.

Let's consider some general recommendations before going into detail on
specific sections. Here are eight "do's" and "don'ts":

1. Do keep the tempo a strict *Largo appassionato* throughout the entire
    Prelude. A broad, 3-beat pattern will help. Another suggestion is to
    think a few measures in $\frac{3}{2}$ rather than $\frac{3}{4}$ which will be a psychologi-
    cal shift from quarter notes to half notes as the basic beat.

2. Don't let the trombones and tuba become too heavy; they can play
    solidly and firmly, yet with a very legato tone.

3. Don't take the *Allegro* in the *Fugue* too literally. Holding back a bit
    will make it easier to play each note clearly.

4. Emphasize the trills. These were one of Handel's specialties; in fact,
    this is one way of identifying his music.

5. Pay close attention to the accent marks that are found throughout the
    work.

6. In the *Fugue*, each entrance of the exposition should be positive and
    played with confidence. If necessary, subdue a bit at the end of a
    section in order to allow the next "voice" to be heard as it enters.

7. Avoid using the cued parts unless you do not have that particular
    instrument.

8. For the most part, the terraced dynamics of the baroque must be

---

*George Frederic Handel. *Prelude and Fugue in D Minor*. Freely Transcribed for Orchestra by Hans
Kindler. Copyright Belwin-Mills Publishing Corp., Melville, N.Y., 11746. 1950. Used by permission.

adhered to. However, toward the end of the baroque era (mid-18th Century) some use of the *crescendo* and *decrescendo* was made, and Dr. Kindler has included some such indications.

Now let's observe the composition, as they say in the profession, "from the top."

Prelude

You will notice that the triplet figure makes up the moving part in the entire *Prelude*. This figure often presents problems to young players—they may tend to cut the last note short, hurry all the notes, or make a slight pause after each group. Work carefully on this. The strings may have more trouble than the winds.

Notice how the arranger has bowed the strings, beginning with the first measure (Figure 13-1a). The reason for this is that a down-bow can then be

Figure 13-1a

taken on the first beat of measure two. At the end of the first beat it will be necessary to take another down-bow for the second beat; this will insure that a break is made before beat two.

If the passage were bowed as in Figure 13-1b the tendency would be to give undue pressure on the up-bow on the first beat of the second measure in order to bring the bow up to the frog in preparation for the attack on beat two. By using Hans Kindler's bowing, the smoothness on the first beat of measure two will be assured and a break must occur after beat one, since the bow will be off the string in preparation for beat two.

Figure 13-1b

I have tried both types of bowings (Figures 13-1a and 13-1b) and have found that in using the latter, some players will usually forget to break clean after the up-bow quarter note of beat one.

Be sure to observe the dash under the quarter note in all measures. The tendency will be to make this almost an eighth note in order to have time for the return bow (off the string) in preparation for the second beat. Give each quarter note the full beat. Remind your players that in *largo* tempo there is enough time for changing the bow, especially since the tenuto indication gives leeway for a broader beat. Don't let the eighth note in measure two be too short; again, broaden this out just a bit.

The triplets on the second beat of measure one should be started at the frog, using the lower half of the bow. Then on beat three about two-thirds of the bow should be used so that a little more will be available for the last two notes. If this is not done, these two notes tend to become staccato because there is not enough bow to give them a broad feeling; also, they can be rushed.

Maintain this system of bowing in all similar passages unless otherwise indicated. It will be worthwhile to take the strings through this section alone before working with the full orchestra.

At the beginning, the cellos are in unison with the upper strings. This puts their part quite high, but it is not unduly difficult if the fingerings in Figure 13-1c are used.

Having discussed the first few measures with reference to the strings, we'll now proceed to the other sections. These measures are very important —they set the style for the entire *Prelude*.

When the *tutti* comes on the second beat of the second measure, hold back on dynamics. It is only *forte*; save the *ff* for one measure after C. Keep the brass down to allow the woodwinds to be heard as a choir.

Go over the illustration in Figure 13-1d several times in order to obtain the exact length of the eighth note.

Figure 13-1c

Figure 13-1d

The timpani player should be careful not to overpower. Many young percussionists tend to play too loud, especially if they are accustomed to playing in stage bands or rock groups.

Proceeding on into the next part, we see that the woodwinds and strings are together on the triplets two measures before B. All the notes here are marked with accents, but if the first of each group of three is given a slight attack, it will help keep them together. The string players will have to push a little harder when the triplet begins on the up-bow. The bow strokes should be martelé style.

In the measure before B, hold back the *crescendo* in the horns, trumpets, and trombones to allow the triplet figure in the bassoons, bass clarinet, and lower strings to be heard. The full impact of the *crescendo* does not come until the third beat of the following measure.

At letter B, there is an awkward spot for oboe, clarinet, bassoon, and upper strings. Observe that the first short note is a sixteenth, the last an eighth. It is an easy mistake for students to play all the notes following the rest almost as eighths. The oboe and clarinet may not have trouble, but the strings might, because of bowing problems.

Have the violins and violas play the sixteenth note at the frog—*on the string*. They should lift the bow after the dotted quarter and take a short up-bow near the frog on the eighth.

The cello and bass players need only stop the bow before playing the sixteenth note. Also, their *crescendo* will be easy, since it is on the up-bow. (Don't take the slur on the last two notes in the previous measure this time.) The quarter note then will be on a firm down-bow.

The bassoon part may be a bit tricky for high school players; a little work with cello, bass, and bassoon (and bass clarinet if you have one) may be necessary for precision on these two measures.

At letter D, you may want just two horns for the first two measures, then have the others join. (For all points mentioned from letter D to the end of the *Prelude*, see Figure 13-1f, p. 198.) If you have only two horns in the orchestra, they will have to start *piano* and increase in volume. This is a very important passage for them. There will probably be no need to hold back the volume on the half notes to allow the triplet figure by the first and second violins to come through—it will still be heard. (This is really a continuation of the figuration begun by the horns.) The viola and cello have the same figure as the horns (except for the cello going to the octave on the last beat of each measure). This adds color, but the horns will and should predominate.

After starting the passage *piano*, raise the dynamic level each measure rather than attempting a smooth and even *crescendo* on each half note. The listener will not be aware that the *crescendo* is done stepwise:
⌐⌐⌐ but will hear it as a gradual process.

At D, the violins have a tenuto on the first beat, calling for considerable down-bow, yet the players will need to begin working their way up toward the frog again so that by the end of the measure they will have a full bow with which to begin the next measure. Students often fail to do this because they don't look far enough ahead and get caught at the upper part of the bow. This sequence (here is a good time for them to learn this term) goes up in pitch, which psychologically helps the *crescendo* in each succeeding measure.

The cello part, while going up on the A string, is really not too difficult. It is situated well and goes up stepwise. In the fourth measure of D, using the following fingering will aid in adding volume to the high B flat (Figure 13-1e). Using the third finger on the B flat produces a clearer tone than the weaker fourth.

In the third measure from the end, while no *ritard* is indicated, a slight

Figure 13-1e

broadening of the third beat will give a similar effect without bringing the music down to a dragging tempo. The lower strings should use considerable bow on the last three triplets to add volume.

The last eighth note in the measure before the end of the *Prelude* should be held a little longer than usual to bring out the dissonance in anticipation of the final chord (a device often used in baroque music). This lengthening of the note gives time to add to the *crescendo*. (I have the players mark the note with a tenuto line thus: ♩ to remind them.)

On the last chord, all the instruments that have the third should play out so that the major chord can be full and rich. You'll notice that the arranger had this in mind, since he gave the C# to six instruments and the E (fifth) to five (all of which are divided parts). Spend some time on the approach to the final chord and the chord itself to obtain the desired blend.

Fugue

You may want to illustrate the *Fugue* by using an overhead projector and pointing out on the score where the entrances are, what the other parts are doing, and how the development progresses. This *fugue* is quite simple and the themes are easily recognized. The students should know what they are playing and that each note and measure fit into a pattern and are not just some hit and miss notation set down by the composer.

The three entrances in the exposition are by oboe, cello, and second violin. (Flute may be substituted for oboe and is so cued.) From the beginning the subject should be played quite *staccato* and every accent observed. Let each entrance be heard, even though marked *mp*.

If the oboe is somewhat timid, have the flute or first stand of first violins play along for a while (cued in the first violin part also). If the cellos are afraid to play out, have the piano with them at first; this can also be done for the second violins. It is not necessary to establish perfect balance the first few times through; in fact, this is hardly possible until the notes and rhythm have been mastered.

The development begins at letter F. Interesting things begin to happen

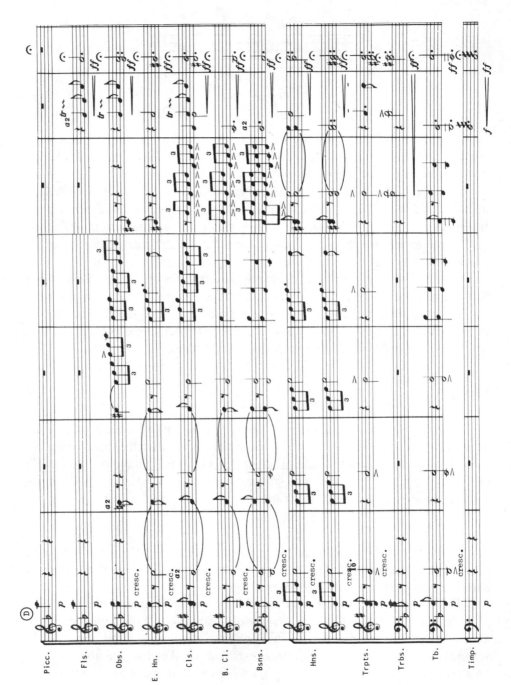

Figure 13-1f

Figure 13-1f (continued)

between the second and first violins (and flute) with the horns adding not only harmony, but also a different rhythm. (See Figure 13 1-g.)

The two basic motives used in the development are shown in Figure 13-1h. Each should always stand out and be very clear and distinct. Play very *marcato* as marked, and be sure to watch the dynamics.

Figure 13-1g

Figure 13-1h

In the third measure after G, the lower strings should take two down-bows on the first two notes to emphasize the accented half note. The violas and cellos should attack the trill on the fourth beat of the next measure. This can be done by a slight accent (quick pressure on the bow with the first finger the moment the note is started). Unless this is done, the trill will be muffled since it comes near the tip on an up-bow. This occurs later and also in the other strings, and should be done in the same manner in each case.

At letter H (and three measures later also), the trumpets and trombones should definitely be heard, making sure that they play *legato*.

The three trumpets have a very *legato* passage beginning four measures and a pick-up before letter K. It parallels the notation in the violins and violas, but is in contrast to their chordal style. The string chords can be played *divisi* for better intonation.

The trombone parts two measures before L should be worked on carefully. If sloppy, the clarity of the same parts played by the bassoon, cello, and bass will be marred.

Beginning with the third measure after L, the bass clarinet, bassoon, and brass players should make sure that the quarter notes on the second and fourth beats are *legato*. This, in contrast to the *staccato* of the other parts, will give the passage depth and make it sound broader and bigger. Also, the *crescendo* will be more effective than if these notes are played somewhat short.

Two and one half measures before letter M, the *fp* by the strings should be executed in a special manner. The bowing comes out so that this is on the up-bow and I leave it this way to allow for the *crescendo*; also, the cellos and basses should have a down-bow on the third beat of the following measure. To obtain the *fp*, the players must attack the note at the tip of the bow, immediately release pressure for the *p*, and then gradually build to a *forte*. They will need quite a bit of drill on this. The woodwinds are also so marked, but the players probably will not have as much difficulty with it as the strings might.

The tempo should be the same at letter N as at the beginning of the *Prelude*. The five measures and two quarters beginning at letter O, although not by Handel, are very effective and I recommend their use. The three bars of sixteenth notes should be played as suggested by the arranger—divide the first and second violins and violas into two groups, one playing slurred and the other separate bows. This increases the precision, yet does not sound slurred nor too detached; a very interesting effect. The ones slurring must attack each group slightly, more so on the up-bow; also, they should make use of the entire bow. The people playing detached notes should use the middle portion of the bow as in Figure 13-1i and have it flat on the strings.

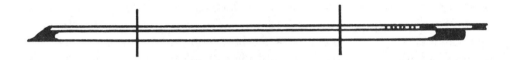

Figure 13-1i

The eighth notes in the fourth and fifth measures after O should be played near the frog by the strings, with almost a hammer stroke in order that each note be heavily accented. Watch the intonation of this diminished arpeggio, especially where the augmented second occurs between F and G#. Try having the violins play the G# (on the D string) with the fourth finger to avoid the extra reach from the second to third finger (F natural—G#). This can be badly out of tune if not practiced carefully.

The *fp* in the brass (fifth measure after O) should be very positive. The *f* will be ample, because they have no trouble in playing loudly. The problem is in getting them to drop to a *p subito*, and this will take some work. Hold back on the *crescendo*; the tendency is to come up too rapidly and arrive at the top too soon. There is usually more time to achieve the climax than students realize.

When the cello, viola, and second violin players get to their sustained minor thirds, be sure they divide so that all notes are played. Also, they should change bow stroke in order to end the *crescendo* on the up-bow.

The second measure from the end should be rehearsed with utmost care. The dotted eighth followed by the sixteenth can very easily become nearly two eighths. The very last eighth note should be broadened to stress the anticipation of the approaching tonic chord. Bring out the third and fourth horns, first and third trumpets, and first trombone (the sustained third and seventh of the dominant chord). The second viola and first cello have the same notes of the chord; they blend very well with the horns and will add to the timbre of the chord in general.

The brasses are distributed very well for beautiful balance on the final chord. The strings should again divide the bow stroke here, finally ending on an up-bow to assure the utmost *crescendo* at the cutoff.

FIREBIRD SUITE
Stravinsky
("Berceuse" and "Final")*

This selection is one that will challenge any good high school orchestra. Some may be able to perfect it for performance, others may merely rehearse it for the exposure to 20th Century music. In either case it is a very worthwhile work.

In looking over the full score, you will notice these important points:

1. You need a good bassoonist. This is a fine opportunity for some excellent bassoon work, and not too often does this player get to shine.
2. The French horn has a beautiful melodic line at the beginning of the *Final*, and this also requires an outstanding player. The horn parts at 17 and 18 are very difficult, but can be omitted.
3. The key signatures need to be carefully considered.
4. There is a harp part that may be omitted or substituted in part by piano, if you wish.
5. The woodwind parts are difficult in spots, with many accidentals.
6. The dynamic effects are numerous.
7. There are many divided parts in the strings.
8. The string players must execute many of the bowing techniques discussed in this book.
9. The first violin part goes extremely high, but in some cases can be played in the lower octave.
10. The other strings go quite high also, the viola into the treble clef and the cello into the tenor and treble clefts. This might be a good time for these players to do some practicing in these clefs, since they will encounter them if they go on in their playing.
11. Toward the end, the work calls on all the resources of the orchestra to bring it to a climactic close.

None of the above should deter you from tackling this work if you have fairly competent players. It will be something different from the standard fare and a good introduction to contemporary music; the benefits to be derived from working on it are numerous.

Berceuse

As the title suggests, this portrays a very quiet mood. This is the reason for the *con sordino* in the strings (except the basses). Herein lies your first

---

*Igor Stravinsky. *Firebird Suite* (No. 41), Re-Orchestrated by the composer in 1919. Edwin F. Kalmus, Publisher, P.O. Box 1007, Opa Locka, Florida, 33054. Used by permission.

problem—to get the bass players to play softly enough. The *pizzicato* should be "stroked," with the hand lifting gently off the string. Even though very soft, a *vibrato* should be used to give resonance to the note. To enhance the subdued, rather eerie effect, *non-vibrato* by the violas is recommended.

At number 1, where the bassoon solo begins, let the soloist lead (within reason). Don't push the rhythm or the eighth notes will seem hurried, especially the last one. Allow the player to broaden it out a bit to avoid rushing into the second measure. Also, the triplets in the third and fourth measures of the solo must be done evenly and smoothly (Figure 13-2a).

Two measures before 2, the oboe has a plaintive melody that must be heard. Be sure the player holds out the half note G for its full value.

If you don't have enough basses for the *divisi* at this point, a couple of cello players can play the B flat and E flat an octave lower. At 2, the second violins and violas must be very precise on each note. I would recommend the same bowing for each.

Use the first desk players on the cello solo three measures after 3 if one alone sounds too weak. If necessary, the first violas can play this part (you will undoubtedly have to transpose it for them).

Note the change of key at 4. The first violins are *divisi* in octaves and the second violas have the same melody an octave lower. Encourage the violas to play out in order to balance with the higher register of the violins. Also, observe the two down-bows in this melody. Take a full bow for the first half note (which really is played as ♩.. 𝄾), then, with a quick movement back to the frog, put the bow on the string and play the third beat. Use intense *vibrato* to bring out the *espressivo* indicated in the music.

The second violins should play *flautando* (like a flute) near the end of the fingerboard and near the tip of the bow, in direct contrast to the melodic line.

At 6, again watch the change of key. Here the strings are divided and the first violins are extremely high. It is best to have high school players all play in the lower octave. They will be in unison with the seconds, but this will not be too much on one part (it is still in double stops). Since the harmony is somewhat different from the progressions to which they may be accustomed, it is beneficial to rehearse the violins alone from 6 to 7 in order to insure the correct intonation.

The bassoon solo at 6 should, of course, come through. At 7, the upper strings should play the *tremolo* near the tip of the bow.

At 8, the oboe repeats the previous motive with some new string effects added—artificial *harmonics*. They are marked *pp*; however, high school players may have difficulty in playing them softly and yet bell-like. One solution is to have them play *p* and move the bow across the string somewhat faster than usual. Also, be sure that the pressure on the round note is intense

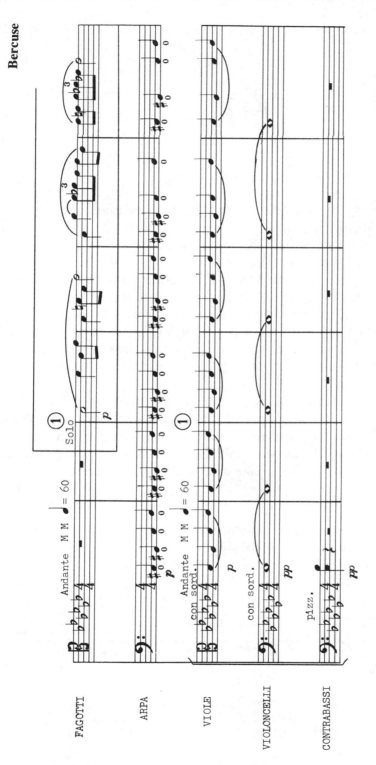

Figure 13-2a

while the diamond-shaped note is touched ever-so-lightly as shown in Figure 13-2b.

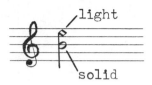

Figure 13-2b

The bowing in the second cello part from two measures after 7 to 9 needs to be adjusted since it is impossible to play all this in one bow at the tempo indicated. I have them stagger the bowing so that the sound remains uniform and the changes of bow are imperceptible.

From 9 to the end of the *Berceuse*, the effect should be one of subdued shimmering. The *tremolo* should be played right at the tip with the bow hair flat on the string; also, it is marked *sul tasto* and *sur la touche* so the bow should be right near the fingerboard. This carries through to 11 or wherever indicated to cease (+). Don't let the players use open strings anywhere in this passage; this would destroy the mysterious effect. Either use the fourth finger or play in a different position.

The treble clef A in the second viola must not be played as a *harmonic* for two reasons. First, it would not sound subdued enough; second, the G# which follows could easily be played out of tune. It is much more effective to use the third finger, followed by the second for the G#. It should be placed against the third finger for accuracy before the third is lifted off the string.

Final

The tempo at 11 (*Lento maestoso*) should be just that. The horn player should be permitted to play this passage in a relaxed manner, almost setting his own tempo (Figure 13-2c). Care must be exercised that the quarter notes are

Figure 13-2c

not hurried, but given their full value. High school students often rush quarter notes when the time signature is $\frac{3}{2}$ because they really think of them as eighth notes. The *tremolo* in the second violins and violas should be played from the middle to the tip of the bow.

At 12, the clarinet part should definitely be heard. It may be necessary to have your player do it at *p* level in order for it to come through sufficiently (Figure 13-2d). It is a good idea to have the first violins and clarinet practice together from 12 to 13.

Figure 13-2d

The trills in the second violins and violas (at 13) should be slightly attacked on each beat. This can be executed with a slight extra pressure at the start of each beat, plus an ever-so-slight hesitation on the bow immediately before the trill begins. This will make each note stand out clearly. While there is no *crescendo* marking here, the players will automatically begin to do so by virtue of the ascending note pattern. Caution is necessary to control this, for the real climax is not until 15. If reached too soon, nothing is left for the *fff*.

At 14, I have the first violins play the top note and the seconds the bottom note rather than divide each section. The oboes should phrase in a similar manner to the violins here.

Just before 15, you may find the group of ten sixteenth notes (eleven for violas) difficult to get even and within the time limit of one beat. Again the tendency is to rush—hoping to get them all in—even if it means getting to 15 a bit ahead of time. The simplest way of curing this problem is to use a divided third beat, thus allowing five notes on each half of the beat. (The violas will have to get six in the half beat; the first half is better so that they won't rush the second half even more.) By giving a slight broadening of the beat, they will have time to play this correctly. Don't be disturbed by the fact that the piccolo part contains a group of seven notes on the last half of the beat. With a little practice the player will be able to get them without being troubled by what else is going on.

At 15, all half notes (except *tremolo*, of course) must be played very *marcato* as marked. Here it is necessary to attack each half note whether down- or up-bow. Naturally the up-bow has to have twice the pressure as the down, since at the time the bow is near the tip. Practice this several times with the strings alone. The winds should not have any difficulty with attacks; have them tongue each note.

Don't miss the *pp subito* at 16. To overlook this is to neglect one of the many highlights of this selection.

The *tremolo* in the second viola part, two measures before 17 should come through. If you happen to be weak in the viola section, have them play it without *tremolo*; this will make the part stand out.

At 17, the time signature changes to $\frac{7}{4}$ which may be new to many of your players. Explain to them that it is subdivided, sometimes 3-2-2 and sometimes 2-2-3, and that you will beat accordingly.

It is best to hold back on the dynamics at 17, remember it is only *ff*. It is a common inclination to give all in a place such as this and fail to save for the highest point yet to come.

The horn part at 17 is difficult, but you can omit it; the timpani and basses provide action on the first beat. The trumpet and trombone parts from here on must be very clean. The long ascending slide in the strings should be played on the down-bow starting at the frog with a strong attack and using a very swift bow stroke to get near the tip as rapidly as possible for the *tremolo*.

Beginning at 18, the woodwinds may have some problems with the trip-lets. This can be because of the many measures involved and the repeated notes. Have the players accent the first of each triplet slightly. Again, the horn part can present a problem. It is usually best to omit this portion and replace it with a concert G (below middle C) to go with the tuba part.

Note that the upper strings are to play each chord on the down-bow beginning with the third measure after 18. These should be played *non-divisi* for a powerful effect. (You may want to divide the few perfect fifth chords because of intonation, but if they can play them without too much of a prob-lem, let them, since it adds to the massive effect to have as many notes as possible.) The down-bows should be played at the frog with fast, crisp strokes,

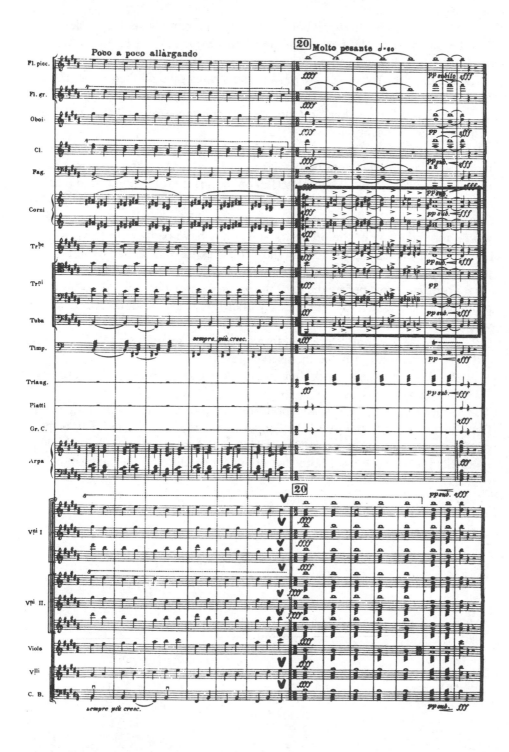

Figure 13-2e

using approximately one-third of the bow; do not try to take a full bow. This pattern continues until 19.

There should be no *ritard* before 19. Here the bowing should be down-up, with broad strokes. The tempo marking (*Maestoso*) gives time to do this, yet each note should be played with an attack (even though only the winds are so marked). Here the dynamics are *fff*. Let the strings give all they have; there is no way that they can possibly cover the winds. Here piano may be used in lieu of harp, if you wish. Don't overlook the importance of timpani, tuba, and string bass in this section.

As you get into *Poco a poco allargando*, broaden the bow strokes even more. The last quarter note before 20 must be played on the up-bow so that there can be a very rapid down-bow (flat on the string) for the *ffff* tremolo at 20.

From 20 to the end, let the entire orchestra expend its full resources. For five measures devote your complete attention to the brass (you will not need to worry about the rest of the orchestra since they have pedal point). Make each half note a firm attack, yet sustain the tied notes for full value. At this tempo there is ample time to allow for each new attack.

Three measures before the end, the *pp subito* must be given attention. The problem is how to achieve this quickly after *ffff*. It can be done in one of two ways:

1. Make a complete break before the *pp* for a second or two. This allows the players to poise themselves for it.
2. Do not make a break, but an ever-so-slight "hesitation" and proceed with the *pp*.

The second procedure is usually preferred by professionals, but is more difficult to execute than the first. The danger in making a complete break is that a player may "jump the gun" and proceed ahead of the beat, so each method has its difficulties. I have used both, the choice depending on the maturity of the players.

Appendix I

Model Warm-Up Drills

The following are models of various drill exercises. All drills should be rehearsed slowly at first, then the tempo gradually increased. These examples can be expanded by using different pitches, keys, rhythms, and dynamics.

The indications are for strings in Figure 6, but these can be used for winds as well.

Figures 7 through 10 are for strings only, showing usual bowings for excerpts from selected symphonic works.

Figure 1

Figure 2

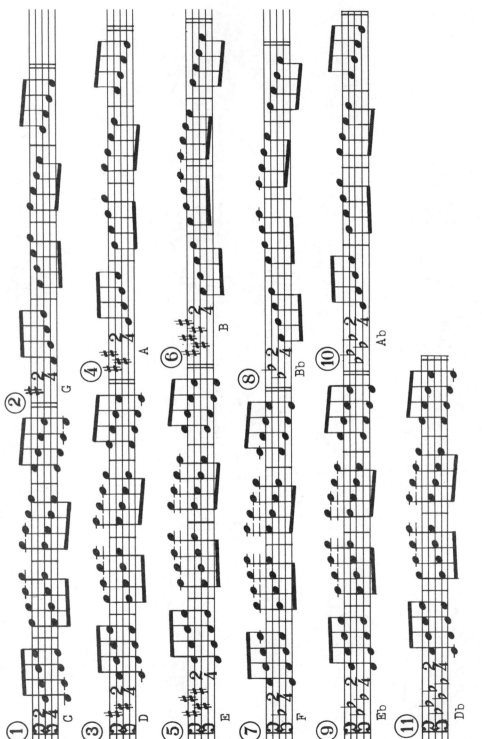

Figure 3

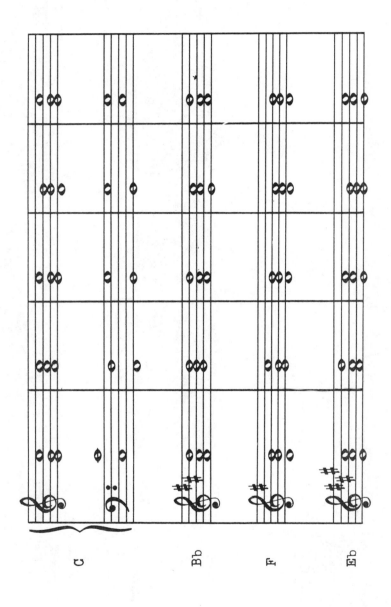

Figure 4

Figure 5

Figure 6

Figure 6 (continued)

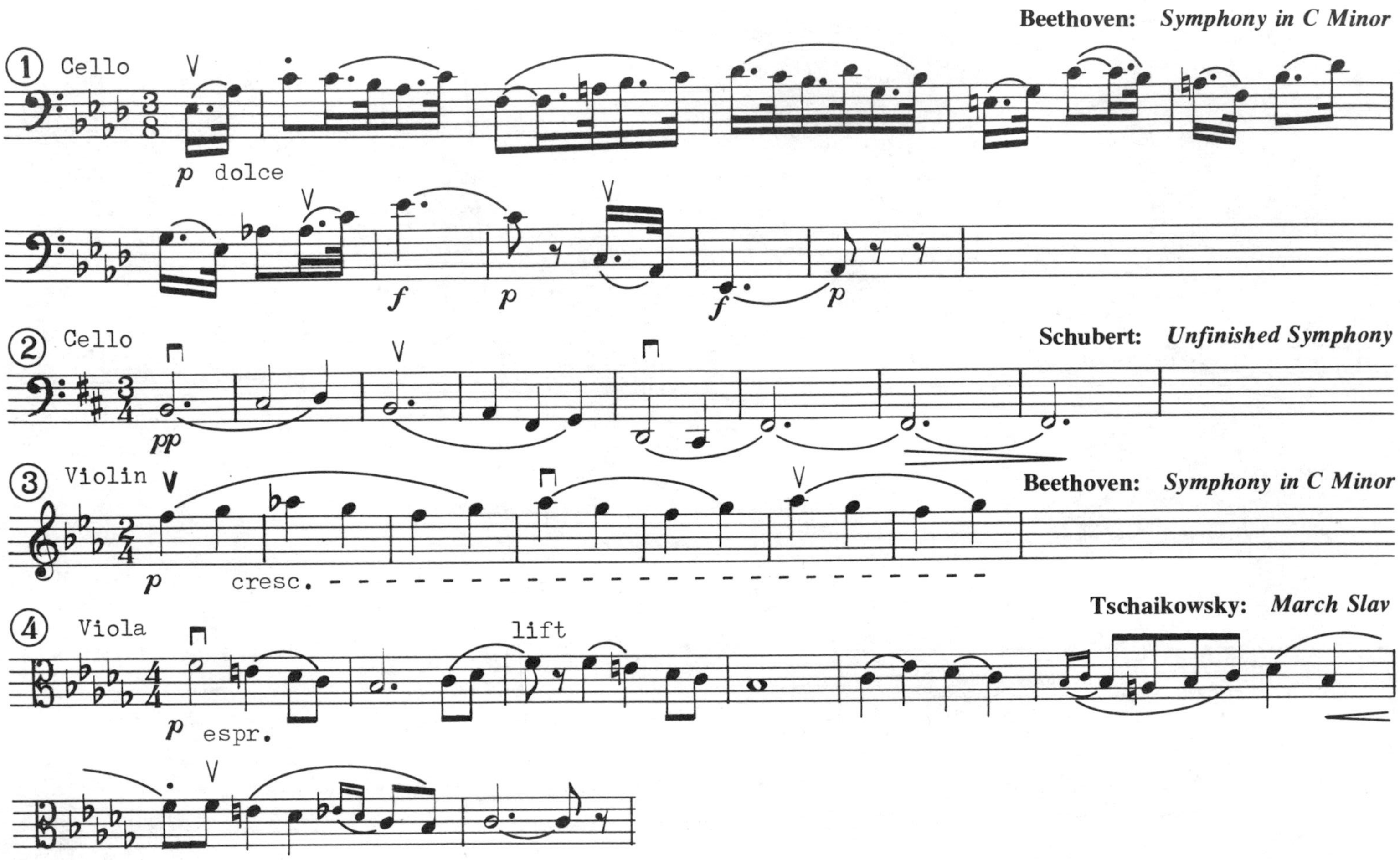
Beethoven: Symphony in C Minor
1 Cello
p dolce
f
p
f
p
2 Cello
Schubert: Unfinished Symphony
pp
3 Violin
Beethoven: Symphony in C Minor
p
cresc.
4 Viola
Tschaikowsky: March Slav
lift
p
espr.

Figure 7

Figure 8

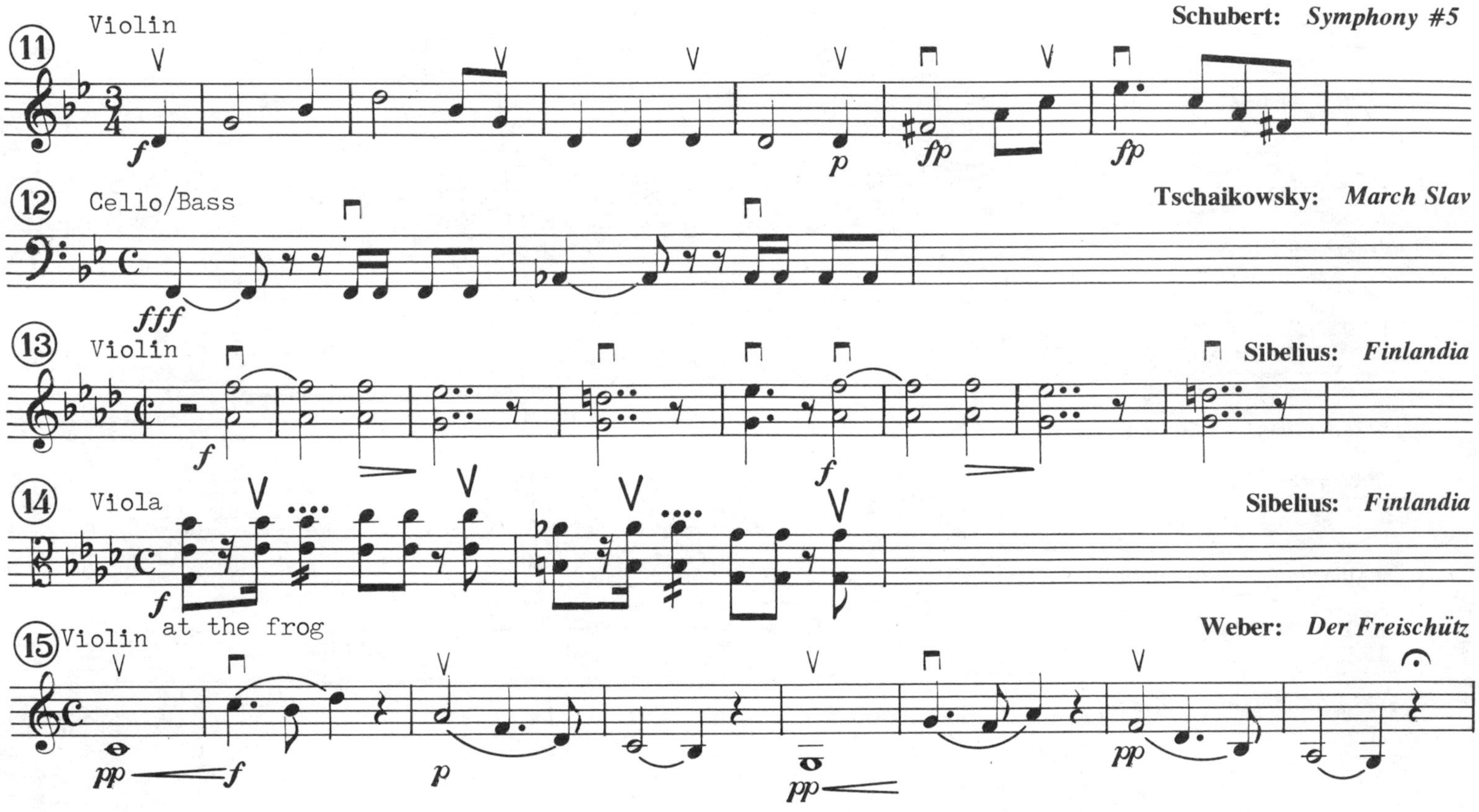
11
Violin
Schubert: Symphony #5
fp
12
Cello/Bass
Tschaikowsky: March Slav
fff
13
Violin
Sibelius: Finlandia
14
Viola
Sibelius: Finlandia
15
Violin
at the frog
Weber: Der Freischütz
pp

Figure 9

Figure 10

Appendix II

Some Suggested Seating Arrangements

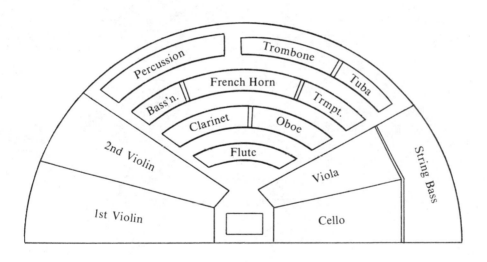

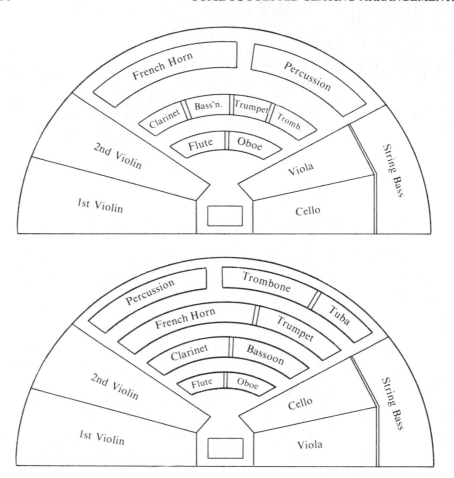

SOME EXAMPLES OF SEATING
FOR THEATRE ORCHESTRA

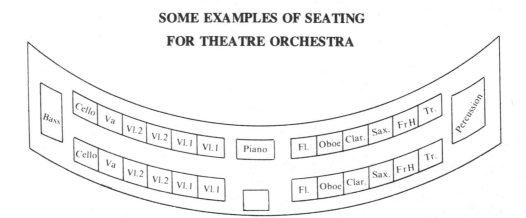

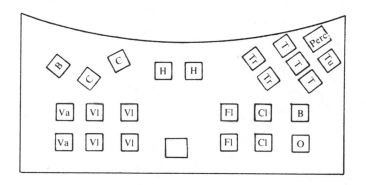

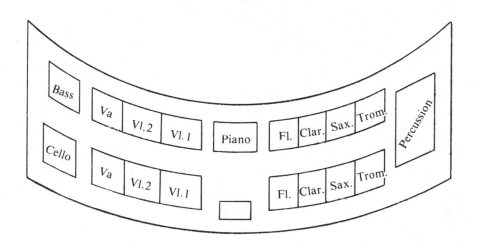

Appendix III

Transposition Table

INSTRUMENT	ACTUAL SOUND
Woodwinds:	
Piccolo	Octave higher than written
Flute	As written
Oboe	As written
English Horn	Perfect 5th lower than written
Clarinet in B Flat	Major 2nd lower than written
Clarinet in A	Minor 3rd lower than written
Bass Clarinet	𝄞 Major 9th lower than written
	𝄢 Major 2nd lower than written
Bassoon	As written
Contra Bassoon	Octave lower than written
E Flat Alto Saxophone	Major 6th lower than written
B Flat Tenor Saxophone	Major 9th lower than written
Brass:	
Horn: in B Flat-basso	Major 9th lower than written
in C	Octave lower than written
in D	Minor 7th lower than written

INSTRUMENT	*ACTUAL SOUND*
in E Flat	Major 6th lower than written
in E	Minor 6th lower than written
in F	Perfect 5th lower than written
in G	Perfect 4th lower than written
in A Flat	Major 3rd lower than written
in A	Minor 3rd lower than written
in B Flat-alto	Major 2nd lower than written
Trumpet: in B Flat	Major 2nd lower than written
in A	Minor 3rd lower than written
in D	Major 2nd higher than written
in E Flat	Minor 3rd higher than written
in E	Major 3rd higher than written
in F	Perfect 4th higher than written
in C	As written
Trombone	As written
Bass Trombone	As written
Tuba	As written

Percussion:

Timpani	As written
Xylophone	Octave higher than written
Glockenspiel or Orchestra Bells	Two octaves higher than written (usually)
Vibraphone	As written
Tubular Bells (Chimes)	Octave higher than written

Strings:

Violin	As written
Viola	As written
Cello	As written
Bass	Octave lower than written

The harp and piano sound as written. The celesta sounds an octave higher than written. These are in a special category since, technically, they do not belong in any of the classifications above.

Appendix IV

Table of Possible Substitutions

There are times when you may find yourself in a position in which it is necessary to substitute instruments for those written in the score. This is perfectly legitimate for high school orchestras, but effort should be made to secure complete instrumentation whenever possible.

Transposition is required on some of the following substitutions:

SCORED INSTRUMENT	SUBSTITUTION
Flute	Violin
Oboe	Trumpet (muted)
Bass Clarinet	Tenor Saxophone
Bassoon	Cello, Trombone, Baritone, Bass Clarinet
Contra Bassoon	String Bass
Trumpet	Cornet
Trombone	Baritone
Tuba	String Bass, Bass Trombone, Baritone
Violin	Flute
Viola	Clarinet

SCORED INSTRUMENT	*SUBSTITUTION*
Cello	Bassoon, Baritone
String Bass	Tuba, Baritone, Trombone
Harp	Piano
Celesta	Piano

INDEX

A

Acoustical shell, 51, 173-174
Acoustics, 51, 186
Adagio for Strings-Barber, 131
Additions (instrumental), 105
Administrators:
    awareness of group, 146
    cooperation with music dept., 17
    conferences with, 82
    help in planning facilities, 52-54, 61
    help with discipline, 139-140
    interest in program, 145
Aides:
    help with ensembles, 28
    help with musical show, 177
    help with sectionals, 24, 27, 117, 129
Air conditioning, 56, 160
All-city high school orchestra, 81-82, 84, 110
American Salute-Gould, 153
Andalucia Suite-Lecuona, 87, 151, 152
Announcements:
    director's preparation, 92, 93
    during conclusion of rehearsal, 112
    first rehearsal, 75, 89
Arrangements, 71-73, 192-202
    judging, 72-73
    values of, 71-72
Articulation, 30, 31, 109
Audition, 29-35 (*see also* Tryout)
Auditorium:
    acoustics of, 51
    already booked, 188
    dress rehearsal in, 182
    performance site, 146
    rehearsal with chorus, 173
    temperature check, 55

B

Bacchanale from *Samson and Delilah*-Saint-
    Saens, 87, 153

Bach-Brandenburg Concertos #3, #6, 131
Balance, 24, 28
    in musical show, 182, 185, 186, 187, 188
    in *Prelude and Fugue*, 197, 202
    with chorus and orchestra, 175
    with soloist and orchestra, 166, 167
Barber, Adagio for Strings, 131
Bassoon:
    in *Firebird Suite*, 203, 204, 205
    in *Prelude and Fugue*, 196
    problems of, 104
Bass clarinet, 192, 196
Bass viol (*see* String bass)
Beat, 104, 170, 172
Beckman, Symphony of Bells, 151
Beethoven:
    Contra Dance in C, 151
    Egmont Overture, 151
Bellevue, Washington, 20, 45-46
    Sammamish High School, 20, 45-46
Bend, Oregon, 20
    Bend High School, 20
Berceuse from *The Firebird Suite*, 153, 203-206
Bizet, Farandole from *L'Arlesienne Suite #2*,
    87, 153
Blank, tryout, 31
Bloch-Concerto Grosso with piano, 131
Boccherini—Minuet, 131
Bohm—Perpetual Motion, 132
Bolzoni—Minuet, 131
Borodin—Polovetsian Dances, 153
Bow, correct use of, 102-103
Bowing, 102-103, 117-125, 193-210
    techniques, 121-125
    terms (defined), 117-121
        a punta d'arco, 120
        arco, 126
        col legno, 120
        détaché, 118
        down-bow, 117
        frog, 117

231